# THE PARTY BOOK

FOLLOWING PAGES: *Christmas is my favorite holiday. Here is the way I set my table for Christmas dinner. Treat yourself like company every now and then!*

# Everything You Need to Know for Imaginative, Never-fail Entertaining at Home

## BY MILTON WILLIAMS

### America's Leading Caterer

DOUBLEDAY & COMPANY, INC.

# THE PARTY BOOK

## AND ROBERT WINDELER

Photography by Ronnie Kaufman

GARDEN CITY, NEW YORK

## ACKNOWLEDGMENTS

The authors acknowledge the contributions of a great many people to this book, but it was Bobbi Elliott who really put (and kept) the whole project together, and for that and much more we are, lovingly and everlastingly, grateful.

DESIGNED BY LAURENCE ALEXANDER

# CONTENTS

We may live without poetry, music and art;
We may live without conscience and live without heart;
We may live without friends; we may live without books;
But civilized man cannot live without cooks.

He may live without books,—what is knowledge but grieving?
He may live without hope,—what is hope but deceiving?
He may live without love,—what is passion but pining?
But where is the man that can live without dining?

EDWARD ROBERT BULWER-LYTTON,
*British statesman and poet*

## AUTHOR'S NOTE

I've mentioned many of my favorite brands in this book; there are comparable brands available throughout the country. But certain products have become second nature to me and my purpose for including them is simply to share them with you. My use of brand names is not an endorsement, and I have not been paid to mention any of them; you can use any brand you wish or any brand that is readily available to you.

M.W.

# THE PARTY BOOK

PRECEDING PAGES: *Any newspaper, not just the* Wall Street Journal, *makes a terrific placemat. Don't be afraid to mix it with your best crystal or china.*

# STOP BEING AFRAID TO HAVE A PARTY

One of my long-time regular customers used to go to a beauty parlor in Hollywood. I never knew the name of it, because every time I or anyone else called there they just answered the telephone with the words, "You too can be beautiful!" I thought that was wonderful, and it is exactly the way I feel about entertaining: You too can cook! You too can give a party!

While the Milton Williams parties most people read and know about are both lavish and expensive, my own favorite food since childhood has been a hamburger with mayonnaise, thick red onion slices, lettuce, tomato, a lot of mustard—and nutty peanut butter. And I go out of my way to make sure that people know that about me. My twenty-eight-year career as a caterer and this book are both based on my belief that successful cooking and entertaining are only *confidence*. Don't ever be frightened by them. There's an awful lot of bull tossed around about cooking and party giving. But to me a party is simply good fresh food, good drink and a lot of imagination—not "putting on the dog." Simplify your preparations as much as possible, with the help of this book, and don't be inhibited by what you think are the limitations of your home.

There is absolutely nothing to fear about giving a party, but a lot of people, perhaps most people, are afraid even to begin to entertain. First, take that false fear out of yourself and, second, don't listen to what anybody else says about how difficult it all is. I don't care if you're going to entertain one person out of a need to reciprocate, or a few couples whose company you enjoy. It's just silly to say "I can't do it." You can! You just have to want to enough. And, like anything else you really want to do, once you make up your mind to go ahead you will find ways to do it.

Naturally, when you're entertaining for the first time and you're going to be doing all the work yourself you should start *small*. Invite only one other person, if you are single; another couple if there are two of you. Serve a simple dinner family style, in two or three serving dishes in the middle of the table so you can sit down and enjoy the meal with your guests instead of running back and forth to the kitchen. If this first party is well taken—which I'm sure it will be—you will gain confidence and you'll immediately begin to think about having more parties that will be more elaborate. Then you can gradually expand the number of guests. After your first party is a success you *should* have another one right away, to take advantage of your newly found flair and confidence. By the time you've got three parties under your belt there will be no problem from then on. You'll have that all-important confidence and you'll be surprised to find that you are actually organized.

This book can help you get to that point, but after that you have to begin to develop your *own* style of entertaining. Anybody can be a copycat or try to keep up with the Joneses. But the really successful party giver is the one with imagination.

Even the greatest hostesses, like Mitzi Gaynor, the Perle Mesta of Hollywood, started small. Mitzi now lives very grandly in a Beverly Hills mansion with her husband, Jack Bean. She entertains often and beautifully, without any help from me. But when Mitzi and I first met, at the beginning of both our careers, she lived in an apartment so small that you had to close the kitchen door to open the oven or the refrigerator. In those days we'd throw an old quilt on a table in the living room (she didn't even have a dining area) and serve up a bowl of fettuccine to our friends. That's still one of my favorite kinds of parties, and one of the easiest to do: you simply have some kind of hot or cold pasta with an Italian salad, bread and chianti. And I still use an old quilt as an easy and colorful tablecloth. You don't have to be rich and famous and live in Hollywood to have flair. All you need are a few basic tools (see Chapter Four) and the courage of your convictions.

# First, Set the Table

To this day, after all my years in the business, I begin almost any party, in my own home or anywhere else, by setting the table—even before I've decided whom to invite or what to serve them. I usually do it mentally, but you should actually do it, especially at first. You may feel a little silly setting your table three weeks or more before the party, but, believe me, this is the best way to assess your resources and begin to build your party around what you already have. If you were going to meet, say, the President of the United States, you'd immediately know that you have to put on your prettiest clothes and your prettiest smile. Giving a party is exactly the same. If you think enough of your guests to invite them to your home in the first place, they are also very special people and deserve the best that you have to offer them.

Get out your best linen and your best china, whatever that happens to be, and put it out on the table—even if it's just a coffee table in a one-room apartment. Fold cloth napkins into wineglasses. Put three pears or some other fresh fruit or some fresh leaves or greenery in a bowl. Perhaps add place cards, salt and pepper shakers and a bottle of wine. Most important of all, even if you have only one single flower, put it in a bud vase—or an old wine or cologne bottle (remove the label first). Flowers add so much to any occasion and it is absolutely essential to have them, whether they come from your yard or the nearest supermarket. Candles are also a must, and they can be anything from votive lights to the tallest tapers. Don't be hesitant to mix up the candles (and candleholders); use tall or short, thick or thin, on the same table.

Light the candles, turn on some music (the radio is fine), then step back and look at your table. It will be really dramatic and pretty. That should give you the confidence to go on. You've hurdled the first obstacle—your table. It looks good, and you can simply cover it over with a sheet until the party (if you won't be using the same table for routine meals) or duplicate it the night before or on the day of the party. With that important element taken care of, you can now get down to the business of your guest list and what to serve.

# Whom to Invite

The only thing I can't help you with are your guests. But they too go along with having the courage of your convictions. For your first party invite only those people with whom you feel totally comfortable. Instead of saying to a good friend, "I'll take you to a restaurant for dinner," why not ask your friend to "come by *here* for dinner"? Or start with a couple you know really well. They know your lifestyle and you won't have to be afraid of making mistakes in front of them. When you do make a mistake (and you will, I still do) they get to know you even better. And it's certainly good table conversation; you can always talk about the fact that this is your first party, in the unlikely event that there is nothing else to say to each other.

When you are entertaining people who don't know one another at all (and don't be afraid to do that, so long as *you* like everyone you invite) it's always nice, as you introduce them, to point out what they have in common—be it a similar job, children the same age, etc. For people without a common ground, you should put out something for them to latch onto, something that will stimulate questions—perhaps a magazine article you've recently read and found enjoyable or provocative. But *don't* use games as icebreakers under any circumstances; they can be lethal, and they are more than a little bit tacky.

Many of the people you might invite to your first dinner party probably wouldn't have the guts to try it themselves. But you'll be surprised at how easily you'll cause a chain reaction in party giving. When your guests begin to realize that it's all so simple, they'll start doing it themselves.

You'll find as you read this book that I am not a great believer in cocktail parties, and if I'm required to give them in my business I really pile on the food so that no one has to go out to dinner afterward. If you are going to take the trouble to invite people to your home—whether it's one person or five hundred—you should take the trouble to feed them. A brunch can be a good first party, but it's an even better idea to start your entertaining with a simple dinner.

# Let's Kill the Excuses

There are three very common excuses for not having people to dinner: (1) I can't afford it; (2) I can't cook; and (3) My house and my furnishings aren't good enough. Let's take (and eliminate) those excuses one at a time.

*"I can't afford it."* Having someone to dinner doesn't have to be expensive. Food, flowers and wine can be both simple and cheap. If the people who look at a cleverly set table and automatically put a price tag on it ever found out how little it really cost, they wouldn't be frightened. Those same people wouldn't hesitate to take their out-of-town guests to a good restaurant. Well, having people to dinner at home costs about the same as, and sometimes less than, taking the same size party to a restaurant. You do have a few more things to worry about at the house—like having it absolutely tidy. (If you can't clean it yourself, hire someone for the day.) On the other hand, you have leftovers when you cook at home—at least lunch for the next day, and maybe even dinner. After all, the first rule of party giving is that you buy more than enough so you won't run out.

A dinner can easily be built around one dish, like a bouillabaisse or a gumbo, with a salad, bread and dessert. One wine can take you through the meal, from cocktails to coffee. It isn't *what* you serve, it's *how* you serve it.

Saying, *"I don't know how to cook,"* is also no excuse for not giving a party. There are places in every city and town where you can buy food already prepared and then enhance it. Takeout chicken can make a fantastic chicken paprikash. Serve it with barley, mushrooms and onions, and a cucumber and tomato salad. Buy some apple strudel from a bakery, heat it and serve it with whipped cream or soft ice cream for dessert. That's a Hungarian dinner. What's the big deal?

# Easy Hungarian Dinner

## CHICKEN PAPRIKASH

16 pieces of takeout chicken (equal to 2 whole chickens)

1 large onion

¼ pound (1 stick) butter

4 stalks celery

2 (10¾-ounce) cans chicken consommé

2½ pints sour cream

4 teaspoons paprika

Seasoned salt, pepper to taste

Sprinkling of sherry

Put chicken pieces in a roasting pan. Chop the onion and sauté it in the butter. Chop the celery very fine and sauté it with the onion until wilted. Add the consommé, sour cream, paprika, seasoned salt and pepper. Cook the mixture into a nice thick gravy. Sprinkle sherry over the chicken, then pour the gravy over that. Cover the roasting pan tightly and cook for 1½ hours at 350° F. Serves 4.

# BARLEY, MUSHROOMS AND ONIONS

**2 packages egg barley (not toasted)**
**16 mushrooms, sliced**
**1 medium-size onion, sliced**
**¼ pound (1 stick) butter**
**Pepper to taste**
**2 tablespoons chicken stock base**

After the chicken has started cooking, boil the egg barley according to package directions; then drain it. Sauté the mushrooms and onions in the butter, add the barley, pepper and chicken stock base. Stir well, cover, and keep warm until ready to serve. Serves 4.

# TOMATO AND CUCUMBER SALAD

**Lettuce**
**1 large beefsteak tomato, sliced but unpeeled**
**2 cucumbers, peeled and sliced**
**Bottled Italian dressing**
**1 teaspoon sugar**
**Dash of vinegar**
**Fresh-ground pepper**
**Fresh or dried dill**

On a bed of crisp lettuce, alternate slices of tomato and cucumber, dividing into four salads, and put into refrigerator. Put remaining ingredients (except dill) into bottle of Italian dressing and set aside. Sprinkle with dill and add dressing when ready to serve.

Buy a loaf of sliced corn rye bread from the bakery. Spread the slices with sweet (unsalted) butter and wrap the whole loaf in aluminum foil.

The barley mixture should go into the 350° F. oven for the last half hour that the chicken is cooking, and the bread should go in for the last 10 minutes.

Put the paprikash on a platter with lots of parsley. (I believe in lots of parsley; but no stems!) Pass around the platter of chicken, the bowl of barley and a basket containing the bread. Put the dressing on the salad, add fresh or dried dill, and you've got a Hungarian dinner for four!

People think that if they are coming to my house they're going to get something special because of the business I'm in. At home, however, I don't try hard to keep up the catering image and I do my entertaining pretty spontaneously. I start the same way anyone else should, by first mentally or literally setting the table. No one can serve a fancy dinner *every* day, but even when I'm serving "normal" things like potato chips, cottage cheese and hamburger, I still try to set a nice table.

If you have a taste for gumbo (as I often do), make one. Here is a perfect example of the kind of meal for which a patterned quilt makes an instant special tablecloth. Put out a big tureen of gumbo, large soup plates (or vegetable serving bowls from the dime store) to serve it in, hot French bread and a raw spinach salad. With dessert and coffee, this is a satisfying, simple and delicious meal. It's also a little messy, but this can be turned into an asset: Take some colorful material and cut out big bibs. Put each guest's name on his or her bib with a felt marking pen, and lay them on the backs of their chairs, to double as place cards.

Because my gumbo has lobsters and crabs with the shells on and you have to pick the meat out, I put a huge bowl of water with lemons in it on the table to pass around for hand washing. (The lemons remove the fish smell from your fingers.)

Once you sit down to this meal you'll never have to get up because everything is there on the table. And that isn't gourmet, it's just gumbo—family dinner, not a delicacy. When I was a kid growing up in south central Los Angeles, we thought it was a delicacy when we could get some of that expensive ham for the gumbo. (Back then seafood was cheap, though now it's expensive.) Although my mother worked as a cook—sometimes for as little as twenty cents an hour—the gumbo recipe I use today I made up myself. It's very easy. You just keep adding to the pot.

## MILTON WILLIAMS' GUMBO

1 leftover chicken or turkey carcass with a fair amount of meat left on it

4 stalks celery

2 large Spanish onions, diced

1½ green peppers, diced

¼ pound (1 stick) butter

½ cup olive oil

2 Louisiana hot link sausages, cooked

1 pound diced smoked ham

32 large uncooked shrimp, peeled and deveined

4 uncooked lobster tails cut in ½-inch pieces, but with the shell on

1 whole cracked crab in its shell

Fish (any kind, but boned halibut is preferred), up to 2 pounds

Salt and pepper to taste

3 dry red peppers

2 bay leaves

4 tablespoons filé gumbo

1½ pounds Uncle Ben's rice, cooked according to package directions

Boil the carcass in water to cover until the meat falls off, then take the carcass out of the water. Add celery, onions and peppers, which have been sautéed in the butter and olive oil. That's the base for the gumbo. Add the sausages; fry the ham and throw it in. Add the shrimp, lobster, crab and fish (which should cook *only* for the last 25 minutes). As you need more water, add it. Salt and pepper to taste. Add dry red peppers, bay leaves, and the filé gumbo last of all. (Filé gumbo is powdered okra and it thickens the gumbo.) Put cooked rice in the bottom of giant soup plates, serve the gumbo over it and just dig in. Serves 8.

Any dinner can be built around this gumbo—or around any stew or soup. With bread, salad, cheese and dessert, the right wine and candlelight—and, of course, the right company—you've got a party.

*"My house and furnishings aren't good enough."* My years in the catering business precede Women's Liberation by at least a couple of decades, and I can only speak from my own experience. But in general, it seems to me, women are still more fearful of entertaining than most men. A man who cooks, even minimally, for himself might put on an apron, call you up and say, "Come on over, I'm making spaghetti." He'll put a bottle of wine on the table, and beyond that he doesn't care. It just doesn't matter to him what others think. He's going to eat the meal he's cooked, so that should be good enough for you and his other guests. But many women worry about what everyone is going to think and feel that every detail has to be right—especially when it comes to her house and its furnishings.

All that concern can and must be eliminated. Your home is what it is, and your furniture, china and silverware (or stainless steel tableware) are what you have. You can make do with what you have, or if you feel the need you can buy inexpensive dishes, glasses and utensils at a discount store. If you like your good china, use it—even for the most informal occasion. If you don't have enough of the same china, mix it up. One of your biggest worries might be that you don't have a large enough set of matching dishes on which to serve, say, twelve people. But you may have been given wedding presents of a breakfast set for six and a dinner set for six. So a simple solution, and one that can really add to your table, is to alternate the table settings, using both sets of dishes. (This obviously works for any even number up to twelve, and don't be afraid to try it even with only seven guests.) Then you can appoint the table according to the colors and patterns of both sets of dishes. Many of us have wonderful bowls, vases, serving dishes and other things packed away that we've almost forgotten we have. Pull that stuff out, and you'll be surprised at how useful it will be when you decide to have a party. You might also have collections of boxes, animals, perfume bottles, etc., that can be incorporated in a table or room décor.

All anyone needs to be able to do a dinner party are a two-burner stove, an oven and a sink. You can be as "gourmet" as you like with two hot things on the stove and a couple from the oven. Of course you can't have a pork roast and a soufflé with just one oven, but you *can* have your pork roast and do an apple dish on top of the stove, which will make the meal work equally well. The size of your kitchen is no excuse. I won't let you off that easily.

It doesn't even matter what your bathroom or powder room looks like, or whether you have matching towels. But it is very important that the bathroom be *exceptionally* clean. It is also essential that you put out a deodorizing spray, some sanitary napkins or tampons, some aspirin and a sewing kit *whenever* you have company—any amount of people. Those are the things that guests invariably need and are embarrassed to ask for. *You* should be embarrassed if you don't have them out in plain sight. Get some nice paper guest towels, scrub the toilet and clean the mirror. Put a scented candle in the bathroom or powder room and light it before the guests arrive. Add guest soaps, hand lotion and a bottle of cologne. Remember, every one of your guests will probably see the bathroom before the night is through, so its preparation is just as important as that of the food.

# Making Your Table Special

I believe that any room, no matter how modest or how grand, can be improved with lots of little things, like plants, flowers and candles (candlelight can cover a multitude of sins). Go to your nearest nursery or dime store and buy little pots of ivy. Or go to your nearest grocery store and get little baby artichokes or small Delicious apples; hollow out the centers and put little votive candles inside the artichokes or the apples as table decorations.

If your dinner is sit-down, buy little Marguerite daisies and put a wreath of those around each person's place. Or put one or two pansies and one or two nasturtiums or other small flowers in little perfume bottles and put one of those at each place, along with a votive candle. I hate those funereal centerpieces that look like they're ready to go on the coffin. People too often figure that if they've got a table for twenty-four the centerpiece has to be at least ten feet long. It's horrible.

Along with flowers and candles, add a little fresh fruit or even some fresh vegetables to the table, anything that's in season. If these are arranged attractively they don't even have to be in bowls. Green lemons make a pretty centerpiece. If the fruit is edible, offer it to the guests. You can pick just anything you have off a tree, a simple branch of something even—flowering or not. If you have, say, impatiens growing in your garden, float some in three different-sized brandy snifters, each of which is sitting on a large leaf from a tree in your yard. In large cities like New York, where there is no greenery in the winter, go to a grocery store and buy fresh flowers or fruit to use as table decorations. But they must be *fresh*—nothing artificial.

These are merely suggestions for making your table pretty. It's best to use your imagination, based on what you have at hand, including inherited odds and ends.

# When to Give the Party

You don't need an occasion as an excuse for a party. In fact, your first few parties should very definitely *not* be on special occasions; those are the parties that you feel you have to give—for somebody's birthday, anniversary, going-away, new baby, bar mitzvah or whatever. Those occasions are very important and should be celebrated and I will even show you how in later chapters. But you shouldn't attempt them until after you've gained confidence and expertise by having a few non-occasion parties. Your first dinner parties should be given simply because you'd like to spend an evening with someone, or to put together a nice group of people who don't yet know each other. And you should plan to enjoy your party at least as much as your guests.

At home you've got your guests all to yourself, which wouldn't be the case at a restaurant. Entertaining is far more comfortable at home; only a lazy person—and the world is full of them—thinks it's easier to entertain at a restaurant. The world is also full of people who have habits like only going out on Friday nights. Those people are so regimented to their weekends-only entertaining that they wouldn't make good party givers anyway: they'd be too boring. Good company is welcome any day of the week.

You should not have your first couple of parties on a Saturday or Sunday night. If you have your first party on a weekend it might well be a flop, because on a day you're not working you'll give too much attention to the party, and you'll invariably mess it up. There's a compliment and an elegance in having someone come to your home, so my feeling is that if you think enough of people to invite them to your house to dinner they should come no matter what night it is. If Monday night is the night of your first (or second, or third) dinner party, then Monday is the chicest night of the week. Even busy people who work the next day will have to eat dinner. But they should have the good sense not to stay until three in the morning.

Now that you have the "right" night (any night but the weekend), the "right" place (your house, apartment or furnished room—with a few embellishments), the "right" food (something that's easy and inexpensive to fix but looks good on the table—presentation is all), and, most important, the "right" attitude ("I *can* entertain"), you are ready to begin life as a giver of parties. Even if you're a working woman or man who lives alone you can have dinner for friends on a week night, because you can do the cooking and most other preparation the night before. When you come home from work the night of the party all you have to do is take a shower and put out the finishing touches, like fresh flowers and fruit. Your guests can serve themselves drinks while you put the food in the oven to warm up. People say that it can't be that simple. But it *is* that simple. Having set the table and done most of the work the night before, you'll be a guest at your own party.

Here is a basic checklist to help you organize your thoughts and to make sure you won't forget anything:

# The Party Organizer

1. Set your table (mentally or literally) up to three weeks ahead of the party, for self-catered informal dinners.

2. Plan a tentative menu based on your available china, tableware, serving pieces and funds.

3. Draw up a guest list, basing the number of people on your existing resources (with perhaps a name or two in reserve in case of turndowns).

4. Set a date.

5. Hand-write and mail (or deliver) invitations, which give the purpose of the party, the time, date, place and your name, plus telephone number(s) for R.S.V.P.s. The invitation should give a clue as to the theme of the party and should *arrive* a week ahead for small dinners, three weeks ahead for more complicated affairs. Suggest dress, no gifts, etc.

6. Plan your décor, tying it to the theme of the party. Order any decorations that may be exotic or have to come from a distance—the décor isn't dependent on the number of people who will attend.

7. Collect and, if necessary, chase down R.S.V.P.s.

8. Now (three days ahead for small dinners, ten days ahead for larger gatherings) that you know who's coming, put the party into action. Write out your final menu and make a list of vendors who can supply each needed ingredient.

9. Stock your bar (see Chapter Five).

*Setting up the hors d'oeuvres in the kitchen of Helen Reddy and Jeff Wald for their tenth anniversary party.*

FOLLOWING PAGES: *At the all-chocolate party for Maida Heatter's* Book of Great Chocolate Desserts, *even the wine coolers and tree branches were covered in chocolate.*

10. Buy non-perishable staple goods.

11. Rent any necessary additional equipment, such as chairs, punchbowl, tablecloths and napkins, etc. (see Chapter Four).

12. Hire maids, bartenders, any additional help (see Chapter Six).

13. The day or night before: clean house, especially the bathroom, order ice and flowers to be picked up the next day. Order fresh ingredients for your menu, to be picked up the next day. Set table (unless you covered it with a sheet when you did it before) and polish any silver or brass that needs touching up. Set up bar, except for ice and lemons and limes. Fill candy jars, put out ashtrays, matches or lighters.

14. The day: pick up ice, flowers, fresh food. Fill ice bucket, check bathroom again after taking a shower or bath. Put slow-cooking dishes in oven.

15. Get dressed. Greet your guests.

*All you really need are figs, grapes, and a basket to make a statement.*

*Easter flowerpots with* pashka *and other desserts, for a table that both kids and adults will enjoy.*

PRECEDING PAGES: *My favorite meal—a hamburger with cheese, peanut butter, tomato, and onion—all gussied up. This makes the perfect setting for an informal dinner.*

# SIMPLE SUPPERS:
## Entertaining with Limited Space and Budget

Y ou don't need sixteen people sitting at a dining-room table to have a dinner party. Formal dining rooms are increasingly rare, even in houses, and virtually non-existent in apartments. The average single person may live in a living room, bedroom, bathroom and small kitchen. Whatever your particular circumstances, you can still have a dinner party, even without a dining table. Serve a one-dish meal, like a stew or goulash, stuffed cabbage or chicken linguine—foods that require only a fork. Let some of your guests sit on the floor; the rest can sit on stools, on the sofa, or stand up and eat if they have to. You don't need to fuss for your friends. The simple meal itself and its presentation (buffet style) will set the informal tone of the party.

In addition to the one-fork main course, which should be served on a large platter—or in a chafing dish if you have one and want to keep second helpings hot right on the buffet instead of in the kitchen—offer a good jug wine (see Chapter Five), some crusty rolls or crackers, a big salad and a wheel of cheese. A plate, a fork, an all-purpose wineglass and a napkin for each person stacked neatly to one side of the buffet table will carry you through until it's time for dessert and coffee. The table itself can be anything from your desk to a coffee table. If you don't have a tablecloth that fits, buy some inexpensive place mats, quilted or straw, to protect your furniture.

Atmosphere is important to any size party, and even if there's only one, a guest should never walk into a "cold" room. There should be some music playing—records, tapes or a local FM station—and not too bright light, preferably candles. For further warmth and a welcoming feeling, put out some fresh candy, fruit and nuts: this is a good way of saying you're happy your guests came, and it gives the impression that you live this way all the time. I wouldn't dream of giving a party and not having candy, fruit and nuts around. They never go to waste, since you can eat them the next day or even keep them for a couple of days in case other guests are expected. With nuts to nibble on, a short cocktail hour and plenty of food planned for dinner, hors d'oeuvres can be skipped entirely.

Your bar can and should be simple. For a single woman in particular, I think it's nice just to put the liquor out on a sideboard, card table or utility cart and let the guests help themselves. It's a good idea —but not necessary—to have a gallery tray on which to put a rather tall ice bucket, some glasses (the ten-ounce size with stems will cover most drinks), and a little dish for lemon peel and wedges of lime. Put out a bottle each of vodka, white wine and scotch, and tonic, soda and a pitcher of water as mixers, and you should hit just about everybody. (If you're in the South or other parts of the country where people drink bourbon instead of scotch, put out bourbon and vodka; in the Northeast you may want to substitute rye or Canadian whiskey.) The cocktail wine should be a lesser wine than the dinner wine; if you are using two wines, build up to the nicer wine. If the dinner wine is red, have a white wine in addition for cocktails; if the dinner wine is white it is okay to stick with the same white throughout.

It is rude of guests to expect more than the host or hostess has to drink (or to eat, for that matter). If the guest does ask for something you aren't offering it's a bad reflection on him, not on you. There again, once you build that confidence within yourself, you will realize that it is perfectly acceptable to simply say, "Would you care for a drink? I have scotch and vodka."

# The $100 Dinner for Ten

When you're entertaining with limited space and limited help, it's a good idea to plan a meal you can prepare the night before or the morning of the party. The meal itself should be easy on you, so plan to have something that can be done in a couple of hours. Here, for example, is a buffet (or sit-down, family-style) dinner for ten people, costing about $100.

## Menu

*Marinated salad*
*Chicken in crushed zwieback and almonds*
*Noodle soufflé*
*Fresh fruit in season*
*Amaretti cookies*
*Coffee*
*California white jug wine*

Only the marinated salad needs to be done the night before: asparagus spears chopped into inch-long pieces, artichoke hearts and chopped black olives covered with a simple vinaigrette dressing. The ingredients can all be canned. While I use only fresh vegetables in my catering business, I definitely approve of canned or frozen goods—or making dishes ahead and freezing—for simple parties given by folks who work all day.

# CHICKEN IN CRUSHED ZWIEBACK AND ALMONDS

1 can or package (8-ounces) blanched and slivered almonds
1 package zwieback
¼ pound (1 stick) or more butter
¼ cup Worcestershire sauce
24 boned half breasts of chicken
Paprika, salt and pepper to taste

Chop the almonds and zwieback together in a food processor if you have one; crush them together as best you can if you haven't. Melt the butter and rub it and the Worcestershire sauce on the chicken breasts. Dredge the chicken breasts with the zwieback-almond mixture and place in baking dishes. Bake for 1 hour and 10 minutes at 350° F.; about halfway through turn each piece over and dab with 1 teaspoon each of melted butter.

# NOODLE SOUFFLÉ

2 pints sour cream
6 ounces cream cheese
4 tablespoons sugar
Juice of 2 lemons
½ pound (2 sticks) sweet (unsalted) butter
6 whole eggs
8 ounces broad noodles

Mix all ingredients except the noodles together in an electric beater until they achieve the consistency of cake batter. Boil the noodles in hot salted water until soft, then add them to the batter. Mix thoroughly, then put the mixture into a greased 3-quart Pyrex or soufflé pan. Bake it for 1 hour and 10 minutes at 350° F., exactly the same as the chicken.

The wine should be on the serving table throughout the meal, after which you can continue serving it or go back to scotch (or bourbon) and vodka. Each guest should take his own dinner plate—which has also been used for the salad—into the kitchen at your request. You then put out bowls for the fresh fruit dessert (whatever is in season and reasonably priced), the Amaretti, spoons and coffee cups.

# Greek Dinner

Another easy, inexpensive and even more festive party is a Greek dinner, much of which can be done the night before. Like the $100 Dinner for Ten, this meal can be done either as a buffet or sit-down, family-style dinner.

## Menu

*Greek salad (olives, feta cheese, tomatoes, cucumbers and lettuce)*
*Hot grape leaves with lemon sauce (can be bought from a Greek restaurant or canned)*
*Moussaka*
*Pita bread (store-bought)*
*Greek wine*
*Baklava (bakery-bought)*

All of the ingredients for the salad—except the lettuce—can be prepared the night before. You can even butter the pita bread in advance and have that waiting in the refrigerator, to be heated up in the oven just before serving. The moussaka should be made the day before and heated in the oven just before the dinner party.

## MOUSSAKA

**4 tablespoons olive oil**
**6 tablespoons (¾ stick) butter**
**1 medium-size onion, chopped**
**½ green pepper, diced**
**2 pounds ground lamb**
**Salt (preferably garlic salt) and pepper to taste**
**½ teaspoon ground marjoram**
**¼ teaspoon orégano**
**2 eggplants, peeled and sliced about ¼ inch thick**
**Flour for dipping eggplant**
**3 cups Ragú Marinara Sauce**
**¼ cup crumbled feta cheese**
**Chopped fresh parsley**
**Yogurt**

In a medium-size skillet melt 2 tablespoons of the olive oil and ½ stick of the butter. Sauté the onion and green pepper until the onion turns a light brown. Add ground lamb, (garlic) salt and pepper to taste. Add marjoram and orégano and mix well; cook for 10 minutes and remove from skillet, leaving the fat in the pan. Add remaining 2 tablespoons of olive oil and ¼ stick of butter. Dip the eggplant slices in flour, then sauté in the oil and butter, very lightly on each side.

In a baking dish put one layer of the eggplant, then cover with the meat mixture. Pour 2 cups of the Ragú Marinara Sauce over that and add the feta cheese. Cover with remaining eggplant, the remaining cup of sauce and the chopped parsley. Bake at 350° F. for 1 hour. Serve with yogurt. Serves 8.

The table décor could be bunches of grapes, which people can eat, and grape leaves and candles. Serving vessels don't have to be fancy. You can double your place mats and put the baking dish right on the table.

If you're in a very small apartment, serve the dinner in the kitchen. Fill the sink with ice and put the wine right in it with a few more bunches of grapes tossed around it. Put the pita bread in a nice gingham cloth in a big basket. Take the moussaka out of the oven and put it on top of the burners, with the plates stacked next to it. Serve the grape leaves and lemon sauce right out of the pot. Line the windows of the kitchen with any wine bottles or jars of preserves you have around the house. Light a few candles, turn off the lights, and invite your guests into the kitchen to help themselves. The effect is absolutely charming and people will think you're a gourmet.

As you begin to entertain you'll discover there are certain basic necessities for your kitchen and your house. You can buy them slowly. We'll provide a list of utensils and serving pieces in Chapter Four. But most people already have things in their kitchen cupboards that they've never seen, and they should pull these out when they have a party. Take stock of your serving pieces, platters, vases and the like before you purchase anything. If you don't have one, you *should* invest in a nice tureen, for serving soups and stews. It doesn't have to be silver. Get Armatale, which looks like pewter and can be put right into the oven. Everything is made out of it, including coffee pourers and plates. It's fabulous, if a bit expensive.

You can buy crockery serving platters in secondhand stores, and don't be afraid to get really large ones. It's better than having things run off the platter if you're serving sixteen people. If you're serving fewer, put the meal in the middle of the platter and fill it out with parsley.

You can inaugurate your new tureen with a turkey soup I made up for eighteen people. With salad, hot rolls and a bought dessert, it makes a filling supper.

# TURKEY SOUP

**2 green peppers, diced**
**4 large onions, diced**
**¼ pound (1 stick) butter**
**1 quart water**
**6 carrots, sliced**
**3 packages frozen okra**
**2 packages frozen petits pois**
**2 teaspoons chicken stock base**
**2 (10½-ounce) cans beef consommé**
**1 cooked turkey breast, diced, approx. 4½ pounds**
**¾ cup sherry**
**Black pepper and salt to taste**

Sauté the peppers and onions in the butter. Add water and simmer for 10 minutes. Add carrots and cook until carrots are tender, about 30 minutes. Add the okra, petits pois, chicken stock base and beef consommé, and stir to melt frozen ingredients. Add diced turkey and the sherry and cook another 20 minutes. Add black pepper and salt to taste. *Be careful* of the salt because the chicken stock and beef consommé are both salty. Serves 18.

If you have a good delicatessen in the neighborhood, another easy way to entertain a dozen or more at dinner is to buy a big piece of corned beef, put it on a board and slice it down. Serve it with hot mustard, a big mixed salad, and sweet and sour cabbage.

# SWEET AND SOUR CABBAGE

**2 medium-size onions, chopped fine**

**¼ pound (1 stick) butter**

**½ green pepper**

**2 No. 2 cans Libby sauerkraut**

**1 No. 2 can tomato purée**

**¾ cup brown sugar**

**½ pound white raisins**

**½ cup white vinegar**

**1 cup dried apricots, cut in half**

**Juice of 1 lemon**

**¼ cup Worcestershire sauce**

**2 tablespoons A-1 sauce**

**Seasoned salt and coarse ground pepper to taste**

In a two- or three-quart pot brown onions in the butter, grating in the green pepper. Cook over medium heat for about 5 minutes. Add sauerkraut, mix well, then add remaining ingredients. Mix thoroughly. Cook over low to medium heat for 1½ hours, stirring occasionally. Add seasoned salt and coarse ground pepper to taste. Serves 12.

For a self-serve appetizer, set several little sauce dishes surrounded by chicory on a big round platter. In one dish put pickled herring, in another olives, in another deviled eggs. Fill one with smoked cod, another with salmon. Except for the eggs, everything comes straight from the delicatessen.

In general, an appetizer is a first course, whether served at the table or not, and is essential to any dinner party. Hors d'oeuvres, on the other hand, are served during the cocktail hour, and I fight with my customers all the time not to have too many and not to make them too elaborate. If you've got a dinner prepared, salted nuts are all you need to get your guests through drinks. You don't want them to fill up before they sit down (on the floor or elsewhere) to your delicious meal.

A small cabbage hollowed out and filled with a dip mixed from a package makes a colorful appetizer: stand raw green beans up in the cabbage leaves to put into the dip. People will say, "My God, that's gorgeous." You can also key your appetizer to the nationality of the party you're doing. For an Italian dinner, put out a tray of Italian salami and cheese and bread sticks on a little table, say a lamp table, and let people help themselves. But keep any hors d'oeuvres (or predinner appetizers) simple, and serve only a few. A good dinner is ruined by too many; you want your guests to be hungry when they get to the table. The only time you should ever do elaborate hors d'oeuvres is when the party is cocktails only.

Table decorations are essential, even for the simplest dinner party. But they can be very inexpensive, especially if you use fresh vegetables and fruit, and candles and greens as mentioned in Chapter One. For autumn, use a few colorful leaves and a hubbard squash. Hollow out the squash and put three carnations in it. Take another little hollowed-out squash and put the candles in it. Sprinkle some assorted unshelled nuts down the table; it's no trouble and very little cost, but people think it's beautiful because they never thought to do it. You've eliminated the florist, normally a very big expense in party giving.

Another thing you can do to enhance your table at a sit-down dinner is to serve each guest an individual bottle of wine set on a trivet. Then you can save those bottles, and for your next party put one flower in each bottle at each place. The time after that you can use the bottles as your invitations, covering the label with the information as to time and place. Deliver them by hand. It's effortless, and shows flair on three separate occasions.

Until you get into serious entertaining it's best to serve one wine throughout dinner. Start serving it with cocktails and carry it through to dessert. It isn't how many wines you serve, it's how you serve them. Which could even be in plastic glasses, to save yourself washing. Put the names of your guests on in Magic Marker, hand them out and say, "Here's your glass—all night long."

To save further washing, I don't even mind using big plastic plates. (I do draw the line, however, at paper plates and napkins in a private home—except, perhaps, for a picnic out of doors—no matter how tight your budget.) But even if you use proper china plates you can simplify the washing-up process by asking your guests to bring their own plates and silverware back into the kitchen after they've eaten, and to stack the plates and put the silver in a little soaking basket. Your kitchen's already reasonably tidy—even if you've served the dinner there—because you did the bulk of the work the night before or that morning.

If you're giving this party by yourself or there are just two of you, there is plenty that you can politely ask your guests to do to help out. If some offer to help with the dishes, let them. They know that you have no help, and they're all just sitting there. You can say, "Honey, would you help me pick up these plates while I put the dessert out?" I would even go so far as to say, "I did all the cooking, y'all can be the waiters. Take your plates into the kitchen, serve yourselves, and come back in here and sit down." You'll find that they enjoy it. Everybody hangs a little looser and it certainly makes it easier for you.

In a very nice way, be a bossy host. Tell people it's all there, and to help themselves. People love it. You have to keep injecting that tone throughout the evening; but most hosts are too frightened to do it. Again, confidence is the key. You can stand with a coffeepot in your hand and say to each of your guests, "Put out your cup so I can pour you some." They do that on airplanes, don't they? You're not trying to prove anything, after all. You just want to show your friends that you've got good taste and that you're trying to entertain as best you can.

For an informal dinner for up to sixteen people, it really isn't necessary to provide any games or other planned diversions. But, as I mentioned in Chapter One, there *are* a few things that could be around the room for your guests to look at, like books and magazines that perhaps would be there anyway. If people pick up one of the books it doesn't mean they're being rude, it's because they're interested in you and in how you live and what you read. And the magazines, whether you've read them or not, can be a starting point for conversation, which is the key to any really successful party.

An exception to the no-games policy might be a luncheon party like the one I did for a group of women who went to parties all the time and were bored with the same old thing. I brought in a lot of backgammon sets, and teachers to teach the women how to play. They didn't know I was going to do that, but they loved it, and most of them later took up backgammon.

For a more festive occasion, you might hire a musician of some kind, or a palm reader or fortune-teller. But those are just embellishments and not really necessary, even with larger groups. For a dinner party given by a single person (or a couple) for up to sixteen, the music should be in the background only, and the entertainment should consist of the food, the décor and the guests themselves. Above all, don't pull out family photograph albums or show slides of your trip abroad. That's distasteful and boring.

Do be yourself and give your best, and your first simple dinner party will give you that confidence to go on. The chapters that follow will give you a more involved game plan for entertaining.

**3**

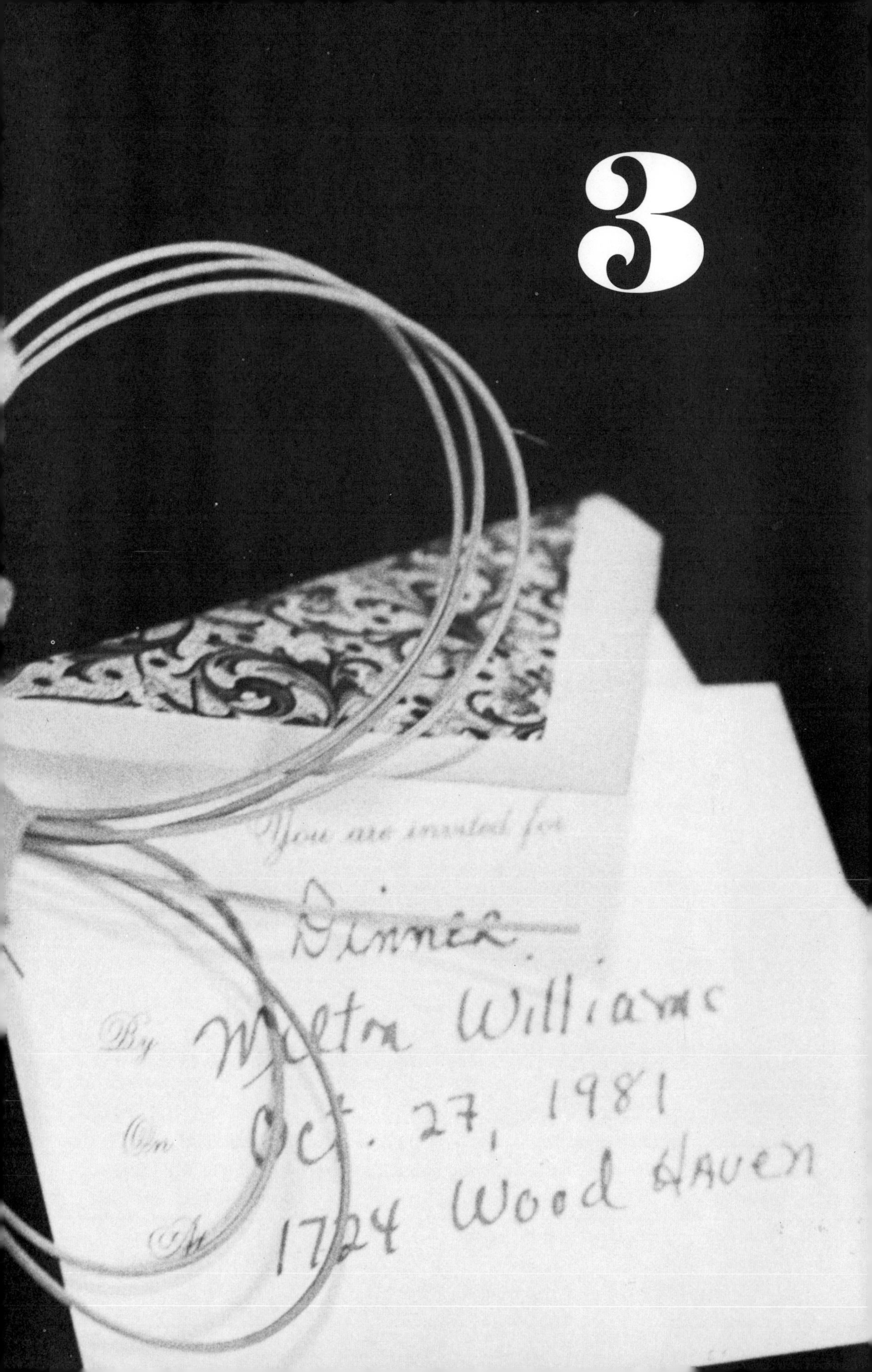

*You are invited for*

*Dinner*

*By* Milton Williams

*On* Oct. 27, 1981

*At* 1724 Wood Haven

PRECEDING PAGES: *Here is one idea for a lovely invitation. Who would want to miss this party? Use your invitation to introduce the theme or atmosphere of your party.*

# INVITATIONS:
## Whom to Invite and How

**O**nce you've decided to give a dinner party and have figured out how many people will fit realistically into your budget and your living space, how do you choose those people? You all know someone that you would like to introduce to somebody else. Probably you have even mentioned the other's name in passing. Have a party to get them together and say to yourself, "I'm going to invite these people to meet those people." They should have at least one thing in common to talk about, and so should any other guests you also invite to fill out your party. People who have absolutely nothing to say or who are very reserved are better off being taken to a restaurant; it's better than sitting at home and being bored by them all evening. (Mothers-in-law are excepted from this rule; once in a while you have to show certain people what you can do.)

At a party you always want happy people around you. Most people know instinctively who relates well to them. You should be sure that these people will enjoy each other because you have found something nice in each of them, or you wouldn't have invited them in the first place. That's the important rule of thumb: Invite to your parties only those people that you yourself enjoy being around.

Don't put people from the same profession together; for example, because you have a mechanic (or at most two) coming, don't invite more mechanics. Mechanics would mostly be a bore to other mechanics. Don't even assume that because two people are doctors they have something to talk about with each other. It isn't necessarily so. You naturally do invite husbands and wives to come together, but for God's sake, always mix them up after they get there, by seating them with other partners.

Except for the closest of personal friends, don't invite people from your office—unless it's an office party, and then you should have *everyone* from the office. But if you have just one or two people from the place you work there will always be somebody who will hear about the party later and ask, "Why wasn't I invited?" Also, parties at which a few people are from the same office and others aren't end up unbalanced: you'll probably find a group off in a corner talking office gossip, and even worse, others who are conducting business at your party! Everyone else will feel left out. If you must invite a good friend from work, be sure he or she has something else to talk about and knows how to leave business out of a pleasurable evening.

# Inviting by Telephone or by Note?

Even in this age of the telephone, I believe in the personal touch when it comes to invitations to a party. Since you are doing your guests the honor of inviting them to your home, it's preferable to buy some cute little note paper, sit down at a desk or table and write out all your invitations by hand. This would apply to any party other than a formal party or one for more than fifty people. All formal parties should begin with engraved (or at least raised-letter printed) invitations. For any non-formal party of *more* than fifty guests, the invitations should be printed. But no matter what size the party or how informal, under no circumstances whatsoever should you buy preprinted invitations at a stationery store and fill in the blanks. Never!

Whenever there is time, you should take the trouble to write out your invitations by hand. In general an invitation should include a pleasant opening, the type of party (cocktail, dinner), the day, date and time. Then put your address (or that of the party, if it will not be at your home); your name; then any special information, such as that it's a fifteenth wedding anniversary, etc. It is also perfectly proper to include the mode of dress (blue jeans, semi-formal, etc.). You will save yourself several phone calls answering questions about what to wear. If gifts are all right, say nothing, but if gifts are not wanted, say right on the invitation something like "We want your presence but please not your presents."

Most important, request an R.S.V.P., and remember to write in your home telephone number and your office telephone number if you won't be home a lot and your boss doesn't mind. It's even okay to say "If you get no answer, please call again" or "Call between the hours of 6:00 and 10:00 P.M." After all, it is *absolutely* essential that you know how many people are coming before you can carry out the rest of the party. Don't be afraid to call up those you haven't heard from and ask them point-blank if they've received your invitation and whether or not they plan to attend. You can be polite about it, using a phrase such as "The mails being what they are these days, I just wondered if you had gotten my invitation yet. . . ."

The slowness of today's mail service is a legitimate problem, and if all of your guests are local, I would have the invitations hand-delivered to arrive no later than one week before the party, for a simple dinner. Deliver the invitations yourself, or consider hiring the neighborhood newspaper boy to do it.

There is no definite timetable for the delivering of invitations, but some logistic rules do prevail. In special circumstances, such as an old friend coming to town on very short notice, there's nothing wrong with telephoning your guests even the day before the intended party and saying, "We're having a little dinner party and I'd like you to come meet someone."

If the party is to be a formal or gift-giving occasion, three weeks is a good amount of time for your guests to have their invitations in hand; this gives them time to buy a dress or a present. In some cases you may have to mail your out-of-town invitations up to five weeks ahead of the actual date of the party—you should for all formal events.

If you are extremely nervous about R.S.V.P.s—and everything does depend on them—you may want to enclose a self-addressed, stamped envelope and a preprinted card that says:


Mr. and Mrs. _____ will _____
                         will not _____
be able to attend the dinner party in honor of _____


You should *always* enclose a reply card for any party involving more than fifty guests; not to enclose a return card is as passé as not wearing pants to church. Formal parties of any size these days require them.

The theme of your party starts with the invitation. For any big party that I cater, an original invitation is the number-one priority. For even the most casual gathering the invitation is its first impression. It should make people want to come to your party as soon as they see it, as well as provide all the necessary information. The invitation should be a clue to the style of the party and begin to set the theme. You'll be using your own imagination, but here are a few examples:

For a L'il Abner party, send invitations written on a brown paper bag tied with corn silk and a corncob pipe. Serve "Lower Slobbovia Stew" (any beef stew with the addition of turnips), and "Daisy Mae Cobbler" (any apple cobbler).

If you want to have a special baby shower for a girl friend you might invite the men to it. This in itself immediately adds a different twist. Buy tiny bottles of Italian wine, chianti for example, with little basket-weave bottoms. Write out notes on colorful paper to tie to the tops of the bottles, giving all pertinent details of the party. Then put the bottles inside brown paper bags, tie them with ribbons and address them. Deliver them yourself, or pay somebody to drop them off at each home on your list. When your guests get to the shower they find that the theme, as well as the food, is all Italian. Everyone will think you're very clever and appreciate all your effort.

There are many things you can do to make creative, eye-catching invitations quickly and cheaply. Cut out a simple square of gingham, write your invitation on it in felt-tipped pen and send it off in an envelope. The quality of paper that you write your invitations on is only important if you are giving a fancy semi-formal party. What is important is that you write out the invitations yourself, and show as much imagination as possible in their creation.

Sometimes you will need to be flexible in giving your simpler parties. If, after doggedly pursuing your R.S.V.P.s, you still get a lot of turndowns—say ten out of sixteen people can't come—try to change the night of the dinner by telephone and by common consent. But if you have a guest of honor who is only in town one night, have the six people who are available, and change the emphasis of your party. You'll have only one table and one conversation, instead of the three of each you had been planning. But no real harm has been done since you are not buying your food or even finalizing your menu until you know exactly how many people are coming.

For a small dinner party, your guests should receive their invitations a week before; then give a day or two to answer. Three days ahead is still plenty of time to reshuffle your seating arrangements and to pare down your shopping list if necessary. Inviting people to a small dinner party two weeks ahead is just too long. That gives *you* too much time to worry about your party; you'd end up talking to other people and asking their advice on what to serve. That is exactly what you don't want to do: you'll get confused and nervous, and even more important, it wouldn't really be your party if you collected ideas from others. You are much better able to "psych" yourself with just a one-week deadline.

Don't discuss your party with anyone, not even your best friend. Don't even say that you are going to cook the food yourself; if you do, that's going to be the surprise. If you can't, at the last minute, then no harm is done. Let your guests arrive curious about it all. Above all, don't ask your guests what they want to eat or tell them what you're thinking of serving. The more people you talk to about the party the more confused you're going to be.

Don't even confuse the invitation with whether or not you are going to cook the meal. For a small dinner party, all you've said on the invitation is "Please join me for dinner." But you may find that you have an unusually busy week or have to go out of town unexpectedly and lose most of your preparation time. It's too late to cancel the party, so everyone meets for a glass of wine at your house and then you take them on to a restaurant for dinner. This flexibility is totally appropriate in such circumstances, but in the case of a larger theme gathering a cancellation or postponement is obviously in order.

Invitation Checklist:

1. For two to eight people, with a sudden guest of honor in town only a few days, telephoning to invite even the day before is fine.
2. For sixteen people or more at a sit-down or buffet dinner party, send handwritten invitations to *arrive* one week before the date of the party.
3. For non-formal occasions of up to fifty people, send handwritten invitations to *arrive* three weeks before.
4. For *all* non-formal parties of more than fifty guests, and all formal parties of any size, enclose a reply card with a stamped self-addressed envelope.
5. For all formal parties, engraved or raised-letter printed invitations, to arrive a month or five weeks before.

There are, of course, exceptions to every rule: The party for which I'm best known among my friends has no invitations at all. It's my annual Twelfth Night party and everybody just comes. I don't even count, although I know we've had more than two hundred crammed into my house. I just buy a lot of food. I have a lot of whiskey and a lot of live music. I tell people who want to come, "It's going to be wall-to-wall people, but if you still want to come, just squeeze in." Some of the people who regularly work for me work that night if they want to; the rest come to the party as guests.

When we were growing up, my mother always had a party on the sixth of January because Christmas was her busy season too and it was the only night she could be sure of being home to have a holiday party. After she passed away, my sister would do it one year, my brother the next, and then I would do it. Then I started inviting some of my customers, and because they were my customers, I kind of got stuck with the party every year. Not only are there no invitations, you never have to ask me if I'm going to have it. I will every January 6 until they carry me out.

4

PRECEDING PAGES: *My upstairs kitchen with the basics for any kitchen—and then some.*

# THE BASICS

**M**any women are intimidated by the idea of cooking for company because other women lie to them. They say, "Oh, I've been in the kitchen for three weeks getting ready for this party," and other crazy stuff like that. These women enjoy the accolades but they know they're not telling the truth about how simple preparation for a party really can be. What they're trying to do is to frighten you off if they think you have potential as an entertaining rival. Pay no attention. Have the courage to swallow your fears. (In my experience, men don't seem to get caught up in a cooking or party-giving rivalry. And I have definitely found that men are comfortable in any size kitchen, from the most elaborate down to the smallest pullman in an apartment.)

## The Well-Stocked Kitchen

Many women, on the other hand, think they will need fancy equipment in order to prepare fancy dishes. This just isn't so. As I've already said, your stove need have only two burners and an oven. And you definitely need a sink and a small refrigerator.

Beyond that there are a few absolutely necessary utensils, pots and pans, herbs and spices, glasses, china and tableware. But a good rule to remember is, it's better to build your menus around the equipment that you have, rather than run out and buy more.

# Cooking Vessels

For a beginner or an expert stocking his kitchen I prefer Farberware because of its durability. It doesn't wear out. Mitzi Gaynor has used it for years and to this day carries it with her to all the best hotels, so she can do her own cooking. But any basic set of pots and pans should include:

A double boiler
A Dutch oven
2 sizes of skillets, one with a lid

With a set like that you can cook comfortably for up to eight people. In addition, you need a baking pan and a few Pyrex or other dishes that can be put into the oven. Worrying about things like copper pots and their evenness of temperature and such will only frighten the beginner away. I prefer to have both metal and wooden spoons in my kitchen but I'm not going to tell you, "You can't use metal spoons for certain foods, you have to use wooden spoons." That sort of thing gets into very fine cooking where you're concerned about bruising this or that. We're not concerned with that kind of cooking here. With some of my short cuts, when you only cook part of the meal and buy the rest, you don't need more than a handful—or drawerful—of things:

# Basic Utensils

A meat thermometer (no other kind is necessary)
2 vegetable peelers
2 paring knives
A good bottle opener
A good can opener
A good wine opener
A set of measuring spoons
A measuring cup
2 wooden mixing spoons
1 slotted metal spoon
1 solid metal spoon
3 good sharp knives (above all!):
    1 French knife
    1 serrated knife
    1 slicing knife

A food processor is very, very helpful to an amateur chef. It's a timesaver, and if you can afford one initially, it will pay for itself in no time if you do a lot of cooking. There are many knockoffs of the original models that are much cheaper; any kind of food processor will do.

# Herbs and Spices

Essential spices and seasonings to keep on hand include: salt, pepper, dill, paprika, seasoned salt, dry mustard, basil, Italian seasoning (a mixture of Italian spices available in the grocery store), bay leaves, Worcestershire sauce and cornstarch. That'll cook a man, a cow and two policemen.

When fresh herbs are available use them! Fresh herbs add more bouquet to foods than their dried counterparts and are an extra touch that will add a great deal to your party. They are particularly noticeable in salads or on fresh vegetables.

There are many herbs you can grow at home without much hassle. It's always nice to have some fresh parsley growing and be able to say, "This is from my garden,"—even if the garden is only a window box. Mint is easy to grow and adds flavor to a great many things. But dill's an ugly plant, so if you want a pretty garden, dill won't do it.

Good as they are, fresh herbs are far from a must, and the dried ones you buy in jars will do just fine.

# Glasses

Every bride has a nice set of glasses; and everyone who hasn't been a bride should have at least a cheap set. Nowadays even wineglasses tend to be all-purpose, although the rounder, fuller glasses traditionally have been for red wines, the taller, narrower ones for white. Some people will give you a bunch of bologna about drinking wine and say, "If the wine is good, it's better to sniff the bouquet and taste from a large-bowled glass." I think that's great for extremely fine wines, or for evaluating wines in formal tastings, or for very formal gatherings. But it doesn't apply to ordinary wines in ordinary usage. Except for champagne glasses, which are preferably tulip-shaped (to hold the bubbles longer), there are no set rules about wineglasses. If you want to serve two wines and don't have a formal set of wineglasses, use ordinary water goblets for the red wine and whatever wineglasses you do have for the white.

As a labor-saving device more than anything else, it's a good idea not to serve water unless it is specifically requested by someone. Give it to the person who asks, using another water goblet or a plain tumbler. But if you just don't put a water pitcher on the table, you're ahead of the game right there. Serving water to everyone today is really unnecessary.

There are special glasses (or mugs) for beer, brandy snifters and little glasses for sherry and liqueurs, but unless you already have them, or need them for a theme party or frequent use, don't bother to buy them.

# On the Table

Elegant china and silverware don't matter one bit, so long as you have enough plates, bowls, knives, forks and spoons to go around. Salad can be served on the main dinner plate, though at some point you should buy a set of salad plates or bowls.

Even though I generally approve of short cuts, I would never approve of paper napkins used along with real dishes. Wash-and-wear napkins are terrific and inexpensive these days. You can buy a very good napkin for a dollar and a quarter; it is permanent press and you don't have to iron it. There are some pretty paper things on the market today, but paper plates and napkins are really for parks, picnics and carnival midways. They are also acceptable for an office cocktail party or a children's party, but adults entertaining at home should stay away from them.

It is the imaginative flourishes that separate the successful party giver from the person who merely puts food on the table. The little extra efforts will be noticed, particularly at the dining table. One way to make your table more dramatic is to fold your colorful cloth napkins and put them into the wineglasses instead of at the left of the place setting. Some attractive suggestions are shown in the color section.

If your dining table has a nice finish don't use a cloth on it, just put out the prettiest place mats you can find. Decorate the table with a wine bottle and three green apples (or artichokes, if available). Attach your place cards to a piece of fruit.

When you are using a tablecloth at a round table, use a solid-color cloth as an underskirt, then a floral print on top of it; this creates a tunic effect that can be a real conversation piece. For the napkins, pick a solid color from the floral print. For a 48-inch, 54-inch or 60-inch round table (these seat six, eight and ten, respectively) use a 108-inch solid cloth and a 90-inch print. For a 72-inch table, which seats twelve, use a 132-inch solid and a 108-inch print.

*Table settings* haven't changed at all in over two hundred years, but reviewing yours just before your guests arrive will help you to remember everything that needs to be done during dinner.

1. The napkin is always on the left (unless in wineglass). So is the dinner fork.

2. The salad fork is to the left of the plate, outside the dinner fork, unless chilled and passed on the salad plate.

3. The knife, teaspoon and soupspoon are on the right of the plate, in that order.

4. The only time a fork can be at the right of the plate is when there is a fish or seafood cocktail as a first course; then the cocktail fork goes on the right, outside of the last spoon.

5. In America, the dessert silver is usually brought in on the dessert plate, after the meal. In Europe, the dessert silver (usually a fork and large spoon) is placed above the plate when the table is set initially.

6. Water glasses (optional) are to the right of the plate, next to the tip of the knife.

7. Wineglasses are in front of the plate, slightly to the right. If two wines are being served, both glasses are on the table to start. The glass for the first wine is taken away discreetly as the second wine is being served.

8. Butter plates, with butter knives laid across them, are to the left, at the tip of the fork. But butter plates and knives are never proper at a formal dinner, where a buttered roll or biscuit is passed. I never put butter plates and knives on a table.

There are virtually no acceptable exceptions to these rules.

THE PARTY BOOK

# Renting and Borrowing

Some items you might need for certain parties you need not own your-self. Evaluate the party you want to give, and make a list of its require-ments beyond what you already have on hand. Decide on your overall budget, and determine which items you might feasibly buy and use re-peatedly later on. Chances are you will decide to rent or borrow much of what you need for a large party. For example, the *large punch bowl* that you use once a year, at Christmas, is probably better rented or borrowed, especially if your storage space is limited.

You might want to invest in a *portable bar* if you entertain a great deal. But if your friends are not drinkers, or you have people over only occasionally, it is easy enough to set up a bar at one end of a room with plywood and two sawhorses or other supports.

Entertaining more than twenty-five people at your home would normally mean renting *folding chairs*. Chairs rent for less than a dollar and up to five dollars apiece. But if you are planning to entertain a great deal and have the storage space you could buy that many folding chairs; it can be a lot cheaper than renting if you use them frequently. A great idea for adding dazzle to every party is to have your chairs painted gold. That color will always fit in. (A warning: everybody'll borrow those chairs for their parties, but when they need repainting nobody will have the money or the time!)

For the parties I cater, I usually rent *napkins* and *tablecloths,* but occasionally I have them made up—this is something I always do at Christmastime. I'll have three different sets for that year, and then sell them to the rental companies for the following season, when I'll design something else. I don't want to have the same things the rental com-panies have at Christmastime, because that's the season every caterer works and you're likely to see the same things everywhere. That's just being selfish, I guess. In general, tablecloths are about four dollars up to fifteen dollars apiece.

Last year I did one set in red, white and green candy stripes, an-other in a beautiful red paisley, and a third in bottle-green and red plaid. I rotated them so the same people wouldn't see the same cloth at every party.

Other items you might consider renting or borrowing:

| | |
|---|---|
| dishes | trays and other serving pieces |
| glassware | chafing dishes |
| flatware | barbecue brazier |
| ice chests | Butane stoves |
| bars | candelabra |
| tables | cocktail napkins |
| umbrellas | tents |

Always call several rental companies to get prices before you order; they do differ from firm to firm. Your Yellow Pages are the best source for all this.

# Having Enough Food

As a professional, I am a great believer in the *quantity* of food as well as the quality. When cooking for myself or five hundred others I always buy plenty of food and expect to have leftovers. The same rule applies to successful home entertaining. Offering second helpings of everything is a must; the guests don't have to accept them. The amounts of ingredients I have provided in every recipe guarantee there will be more on the table than your guests will eat that night. The abundance of food will make your guests feel that, as good as dinner was, they haven't made pigs of themselves—since there is food left over.

A question such as "How many hors d'oeuvres do I plan per person?" always throws me, so again I just say, "Plenty." Of course, it depends on the combination of hors d'oeuvres—big or small, hot or cold—and on whether or not dinner is being served. If you're going to give your guests an hour to drink before dinner, have a mixed seafood bowl—figure four pieces of shellfish per person—and have a few relishes around the room. That should be enough for the one hour. Don't load them down, and if you are serving dinner, have no more than three different hors d'oeuvres. Better yet, have just one elegant one, like miniature blinis with caviar and sour cream. If dinner is meat, have seafood hors d'oeuvres, and vice versa.

Since my own preference is always to provide a full meal instead of just hors d'oeuvres, I'm not an expert on the number of people who can be fed from one stalk of celery. At a cocktail party that I'm catering I'll serve little lamb chops, bite-size pieces of chicken, and steak tartare, so that no one *has* to go on to dinner. The best way to be sure you're buying enough is to ask the man or woman in the cheese store the number of helpings in a pound of pâté or a wheel of cheese, and then buy a little over that.

Here is my favorite recipe for steak tartare, which has successfully helped to fill up guests at many a Hollywood party. Figure ten servings to a pound:

## STEAK TARTARE

1 pound very lean top sirloin (have the butcher de-fat it and grind
   three times)
1½ tablespoons Indian Relish
2 tablespoons grated onion
1 tablespoon anchovy paste (optional)
Capers to taste (whole and without oil)
1 tablespoon Worcestershire sauce
1 teaspoon A-1 sauce
¼ teaspoon pepper
1 egg
Dash of Tabasco
Salt

Mix all ingredients together with a fork until well incorporated. Taste for salt, and add if necessary. Serve with cocktail rye bread, toasted or plain. If toasted, I like to butter it first.

A final word on amounts: my principle of providing too much food most definitely applies to desserts. For eight people make twelve portions, and if you know it's that good, make sixteen!

# Measuring Wine and Liquor

It is possible to pin down more precise amounts when it comes to liquor and wine. At a cocktail party, the average number of drinks is three per person. There are seventeen drinks to a fifth of liquor. If you are going to serve two or three kinds of liquor you'll have to know pretty well what your guests are likely to drink. If you have no idea, try to buy fifths on consignment, paying the store only for what you actually use. There's no sense opening and paying for a half gallon of scotch for one person.

It used to be that there were eight glasses to a bottle of wine, but with the larger glasses in use today I'd say it's less. Instead, figure six glasses to the bottle, or eighty-two to the case.

Jug wines are perfectly fine to serve so long as they are good ones (we'll discuss this further and recommend some in the next chapter); never serve rotgut. Since half gallons (fifteen glasses each) are a little cumbersome, it's nice to pour them first into carafes, or even small carafes for two people—or little individual wine bottles that you've saved from another party.

A word to the wise: never pour your best wine for a large group of people, unless those people mean an awful lot to you. Mouton Rothschild at over a hundred dollars a bottle is really for four people, or eight people if all of them are connoisseurs. Otherwise it gets vulgar, and it wouldn't be fair to your purse. If all your guests are not connoisseurs, lesser-priced wines that are comparable to a good Bordeaux are California's Inglenook Cabernet Sauvignon and France's Marquisat Beaujolais.

In 1979 I catered a half-million-dollar wedding; that topped the record set by the Paul McCartney/Wings party at the old Harold

Lloyd estate in Beverly Hills three years earlier, which had cost a mere $400,000. The father of the bride insisted on twenty-four cases of Dom Perignon champagne at $820 a case, and nineteen cases of Château Lafite Rothschild 1966 at a shelf price of $92 a bottle, for his 460 guests. The liquor bill alone was $70,000. The caviar, thirty-six pounds, was almost $10,000, and the musicians—including twenty violins—flown in from Los Angeles, were paid $700 apiece, for a total of $30,000.

# Atmosphere

I deal with each party and each house individually, and once I know a home I can plan a party from memory—unless the owners make drastic changes in the floor plan or décor. If you don't know your own home intimately, nobody does, and *you* have got to deal with what you've got and what you lack. Does your apartment have a view, and is the party organized to take full advantage of that? Are there enough conversational groupings in your normal arrangement of furniture, or must you create a couple for the party by rearranging or by adding borrowed or rented chairs? If you plan to entertain a lot, you might want to consider a permanent realignment of your furniture.

Apartments can present the party giver with added problems, particularly in the East, where they tend to be smaller than in California. But once you have determined how many people you can accommodate standing or sitting, depending on the nature of the party, you can begin to improvise. House plants and flowers can cover or smooth awkward corners. Candles can help create conversational and serving areas, as well as tone down the lighting. If you have no coat closet or one that's too small it is proper to lay coats on the bed. If it's raining, get a garment rack for the hallway outside the apartment and provide a pot to put wet umbrellas in.

With enough space in that outer hall, and some co-operative neighbors (who should always be invited to the party so they won't have to put up with the noise), you can even have an hors d'oeuvres table set up outside your apartment. This alleviates congestion inside and gets your guests into a party spirit the minute they get off the elevator.

Your own costume for home entertaining is a part of setting the atmosphere of the party, and in practical terms it should be anything but elaborate. The hostess who is doing all the cooking and serving herself can wear something loose like a simple caftan, or something she doesn't particularly mind spilling stuff on but is still pretty. That's very much in order at home. She should look as well as be *comfortable*. A sequined gown would look out of place. I see nothing wrong with the hostess even coming into the living room with her apron on. To some people an apron is distasteful; but if it's a pretty apron and it's clean I think it's kind of cute. Your guests know that you have been in the kitchen doing all the work, and it will convey the pride you have in your own cooking. Have the apron made to match your tablecloth and napkins—be flamboyant, and you'll find you've made a virture out of necessity. An apron matching your napkins and tablecloth might be the envy of some of your guests, and the evening's first conversation piece.

Simple things like having enough *ashtrays* and putting them in the proper places contribute to the atmosphere of a party. With so many non-smokers now, one ashtray and one cigarette lighter for every four people are enough. If you know your guests well, you can put an ashtray in front of the place of each smoker.

*Lighting* should not be too bright or too dark; you might want to lessen the wattage of the bulbs in your lamps for the evening, or change white lights to pink. Always, candles should soften the effect. For a house, a dramatic effect is to put twinkling lights in the trees in your yard.

*Music* should fit the mood of your particular party; without being obtrusive, it should be constant. There is nothing like live music, but hiring a musician could be a substantial portion of your budget, so unless it is important to the theme of the party (singing show tunes around a piano, for example), think twice about it. Records can be awkward, because they have to be changed, and your guests might want to get in on the selection of them. Long tapes or the FM radio are better choices.

*Tables,* including end tables, coffee tables and desks and book-cases, as well as serving and dining tables, should be decorated with flowers or plants and candles. (Burn the tips of all fresh candles, so they don't look brand new, and remember to mix sizes and shapes.) Each table should have bowls of candy and nuts, so guests are never very far from something to nibble on.

PRECEDING PAGES: *Grapes and champagne are the easiest elegant centerpiece or side table decoration. It looks almost as good with wine bottles instead.*

# WINE AND BOOZE

**M**ost parties given and attended by adults in America begin and end with a drink of something alcoholic. Although drinking habits are changing—for instance, white wine consumption has skyrocketed to the point where there is a serious shortage of it in many California vineyards—the good host or hostess should always have at least a minimal selection of wine and liquor on hand. Scotch, bourbon or rye, and vodka, along with the appropriate mixes (club soda, ginger ale and tonic), will cover the preferences of most people when it comes to hard liquor. Depending on where you live or who your friends are, you may also want to keep beer on hand.

## Wine

Anyone who plans to entertain at dinner should try to keep at least a dozen bottles of different wines in his house or apartment; even the smallest place has room for that much. This mixed case of wine should be kept in the coolest, darkest place possible. If you live where there's snow, don't store the wine in a room like the kitchen, which might stay up to 70 degrees most of the time. You can always find a cool place, such as under a stairway. In apartments you can try the basement of the building or a closet that is cooler than most of the other rooms. Behind a closed door—away from light and temperature changes—your wines will last longer.

*Italian wines* store very well and are moderately priced. You should include in your basic case of twelve bottles a Soave and a Verdicchio, the top Italian white wines; and perhaps a Valpolicella, the top Italian red.

Inexpensive *French table wines* that could be included are a red Marquisat Beaujolais and the red Château Timberlay, which is very reasonable (you've got to let this one breathe two hours before you serve it). I would add a Mateus pink and a Mateus white to the dozen, and a Chanson Blanc de Blancs and a Vouvray (both white). I'd also have a Pouilly-Fuissé (white) and a Louis Jadot Beaujolais (red). The twelfth bottle should be an Inglenook Cabernet Sauvignon from California. It's as good as a French wine and certain years are excellent; the prices have skyrocketed accordingly.

Other *California wines* to look for include Wente Brothers Blanc de Blancs, a nice inexpensive white. For sangría I use California Zinfandel because it's got so much body to it. Setrakian is a good Armenian vineyard for white wine—a half gallon of their mountain chablis is only about $2.50. I've taken it to big parties for people who really know fine wine but didn't want to go into their best stock. Almaden and Inglenook also have good *jug wines*. If you find a good cheap wine of your own, don't be embarrassed to use it.

Of course, if you can afford them, a Château Margaux or a Mouton Rothschild are tops among *finer wines*. Buy a young Château Latour and keep it for a few years, as a pleasurable investment. Among dessert wines, Château d'Yquem is about the best you can get—it's just like nectar. Of course, it's very expensive.

# Proper Handling of Wines

If you have a bottle of fine old red wine—and your guests know about wine—make a show of opening the bottle in front of them, displaying the label and even passing the bottle around for all to examine. But it's a bit pushy to do all that in front of a group who couldn't care less.

It's better just to open bottles of red wine quietly, out of sight of the guests. Usually half an hour before serving is plenty of breathing time for red wine, though many experts say an hour. This depends on the age of the wine and its quality. Lesser quality and younger wines need more time to let the heavy gases escape.

You *must* decant a wine if you can see sediment in the bottom of the bottle, which will happen when a red wine gets to be eight or ten years old. To do this properly, heat the bottom of the bottle with a candle, then pour the wine into a decanter, leaving the sediment at the bottom of the bottle. Drinking some of those older wines is fabulous—like drinking velvet.

White wine should chill for an hour before it's ready to serve; you can leave it in the refrigerator longer but it won't get any colder. If you're going to leave the white wine on the table it should be in an ice bucket. You can keep returning it to the refrigerator if you don't have an ice bucket—but don't leave it sitting on the table to get warm. Red wine, which isn't chilled, of course can stay out on the table.

At home I have a set of little carafes on a silver tray. If I'm having eight to dinner, I'll use four of the carafes—one for each two people—and just keep refilling them from the kitchen. So all I (or the waiter) have to do is keep the carafes full. If people want to know what the wine is you can bring the bottle in from the kitchen and show them the label.

# When to Serve Which Wine

I feel very strongly that the correct wine to serve guests is the wine *you* enjoy the most. I happen to like rosé wine, for example, which a lot of people look down on. Yet rosé is proper for brunch, lunch or dinner. I can't drink red wine, except for a couple of swallows with cheese. That's my limit. If I have a whole glass, it's like a sleeping pill: it makes me get heavy and sleepy. In fact, if I ever have trouble going to sleep I take a glass of red wine and I go out like a light. I can drink white wine before dinner, throughout dinner and after dinner and feel nothing.

The common rule of thumb, of course, is red wine with red meat, white wine with white meat and fish. But there are important exceptions: pork has a strong enough flavor to be eaten with a red wine, even though pork is basically white in coloring. Red wine goes much better with cheese than white wine.

The cold duck fad is over in this country, and I never did know too much about it, except that it is like a sparkling Burgundy and there are many people who like it. Therefore, it's correct as an apéritif and throughout dinner. You can even build a menu around a sparkling Burgundy or cold duck:

### Sparkling Burgundy Menu

*Duck, lamb or wild game (from boar to partridge)*
*Wild rice with mushrooms and chicken livers*
*Green vegetable in an orange shell*
*Fruit tarts*

# Champagne

Champagne is always correct. But if most of your guests had their druthers, they'd probably switch to something else. I've found that at weddings we go around with trays of champagne so that everyone can toast the bride and groom, only to have people take one sip and leave the rest. I don't even like champagne myself, but it hurts my heart to pour all this $40-a-bottle stuff down the drain because people aren't drinking it. At weddings and other big affairs it's best to have enough waiters asking people what they like to drink: offer the champagne and make it clear that you have anything else the guests may want instead.

One good thing about champagne, if all your guests happen to like it, is that it goes with everything and is the only wine you can have for cocktails and then continue from the start of the meal right through to dessert and after. But there will probably be one or two people in any gathering who will ask if they can have a scotch and soda or some other mixed drink. Personally, I wouldn't do that. Unless it were a real good friend of mine I'd rather sit all evening holding one undrunk glass of champagne in my hand than ask for a scotch, because it just wouldn't be polite. Of course, a good host would notice you weren't drinking the champagne and offer you something else instead.

# More Than One Wine at Dinner

You can have more than one wine at dinner if you want to. The best way to handle this is to have two glasses already on the table. In case there is any doubt among your guests, announce that the white wine is for the fish course (or whatever) and then pass the bottle or carafe down the table. You should have a little side table sitting nearby with the red wines already opened and breathing. When the first portion of the meal is over, introduce the second wine and ask the maid (if you've hired one) to remove the white wineglasses—except for those who would prefer to continue with the white wine. It works if done tactfully and tastefully.

# Wine and Ethnic Cuisine

Your wine doesn't necessarily have to come from the same country as the food you serve. If you do a Greek meal you don't have to serve retsina, which is an acquired taste in the best of circumstances, or any other Greek wine for that matter. I don't happen to like Greek wines, and I would use an Italian or a California wine, or anything I felt would go well with the meal. I do like Hungarian wines, but I don't always serve them with a Hungarian dinner. (Egri Bikavër is a nice red wine from Hungary; it is not terribly expensive, but in many areas will not be readily available.)

But a sangría to serve all the way through a Spanish or Mexican meal makes sense. It's inexpensive and easy, and not only can be made well ahead of your party, it should be.

## SANGRÍA

    **1 lemon**
    **1 lime**
    **1 apple**
    **1 orange**
    **1 bunch seedless grapes if in season (if not, use muscat grapes, cutting each in half and removing the seeds)**
    **1 cup sugar**
    **2 quarts Zinfandel wine**
    **1 quart 7-Up**
    **Ice**

Slice the first four fruits into a large bowl and add the grapes. Pour the sugar over the fruit and let it sit for an hour to draw out the juice from the fruit. Add the Zinfandel and 7-Up. Let it sit for a while, then chill it.

It's best to make the sangría in the morning and serve it that night. Overnight is a little too long, as the sangría tends to get bitter. Twelve hours before the party is perfect timing. At the last minute, put ice in the bowl and stir to dilute the sangría a bit.

You can also make a white sangría with a white wine like the Setrakian already mentioned, or any cheap California chablis. Then you would use only white grapes, but all other fruit and instructions remain the same.

If you start your guests off with the sangría and carry it all through dinner, this recipe will accommodate four people (with six small punch glasses apiece). For eight people, double the recipe, and so on. Sangría costs you very little, and at the end of the evening everybody's feeling mighty good. A nice added touch is to fill each glass with fruit at the last minute, before pouring.

# Cooking with Wine

Wine definitely changes the flavor of food when it is used in cooking. I don't use wine in every dish. I don't use it in veal, for example, because veal is too delicate. You don't want to destroy the flavor of what you're eating. If I do a boned, flattened breast of chicken I put in so little wine that the taste change is so faint as to seem almost nothing. If something is heavily spiced, though, using wine enhances the taste. I do use wine with breast of chicken with wild rice and mushrooms, to make it taste kind of gamy—yet with real game I use wine to get rid of the gamy taste.

Vermouth, sauterne, sherry, various kinds of Burgundy and port are the wines most commonly used in cooking. Sometimes I use wine in custards or make a light wine sauce for poached pears; for these desserts I use a Verdicchio or a Soave, Italian whites. Of course, in beef bourguignon I use Burgundy. And I make beef grenadine with Floria Marsala:

## BEEF GRENADINE

**2 pounds filet mignon, sliced thin and flattened**
**Salt and pepper to taste**
**1 tablespoon olive oil**
**8 large mushrooms, sliced**
**1 cup Floria Marsala**

Season beef lightly with salt and pepper. Heat oil. Sauté sliced meat 1 minute on each side and set aside. Sauté mushrooms for 5 minutes. Add half the wine. Simmer 5 additional minutes, then add remaining wine. Pour over beef and heat to serve. Serves 4.

Sauterne is used most often with fish; it sort of cooks out, leaving just a hint of the flavor. With a poached whitefish or fillet of sole or ling cod sauterne brings out the delicate flavor of the fish without any taste of wine. Take some of that broth and put it into the sauce for the fish, adding a bit more wine and some fresh basil.

Never let cooking wine conflict with the dish itself or with the wine you are serving to accompany it. The most important rule is: keep the cooking wine mellow.

# The Five-Wine Dinner

If you want to do something very fancy you can have a separate wine for each of four or five courses, including the dessert. The David Orgells do this five times a year at their dinner parties. He is English and has a store in Beverly Hills dealing in fine china and home furnishings, the best of everything, which accounts for the magnificent appointments in the Orgell home.

They always have twenty people, eight at the breakfast table adjoining the dining room, twelve at the dining-room table. Cocktails are served in one room before dinner, and coffee in the living room after. At one end of the living room is a navy-blue lacquered Chippendale chinoiserie piano. A pianist, accompanied by a cellist and a violinist, play all through dinner.

If they have five wines, all five glasses will be on the table when the guests sit down. We just keep taking away the ones they've used. It looks fabulous to have all that glassware on the table, and it's a pleasure to handle. They entertain every two months or so.

# What Goes With What

Here's a short chart, showing which wines I feel are best served when; it may seem unconventional and is not the last word. Your own tastes and preferences should prevail.

*Rosé* wine   Anything, especially "pink" meats like ham, sausages, veal, also omelets, salads; most often used for lunch or brunch, but also correct with dinner.

*Champagne*  Literally anything, from apéritif through to dessert.

*Sherry* (sweet or dry)  Apéritif or dessert only.

*Port*  Cooking, and after lunch.

*Graves*  A teatime wine, sandwiches, etc.

*Vermouth*  Apéritif by itself, mixer in gin and vodka martinis, cooking (sweet or dry).

*Red Burgundy* and *red Bordeaux*  Roasts, lamb, steak, game fowl, stews with red meat (not chicken), pork if desired.

*White Burgundy* (and California and Italian equivalents)  Chicken, fish, veal, casseroles made with any of those.

*Sweet white wine*  Dessert only, possibly cooking.

# Booze

In addition to the minimal supplies for a home bar discussed earlier, the complete bar setup would include: gin, rum, Dubonnet (blond or red), sherry (sweet or dry), a red jug wine, vermouth (dry to mix with gin or vodka) to make martinis; additional mixers would be grapefruit juice, Rose's lime juice, Mr. and Mrs. T or Snappy Tom Bloody Mary mix, orange juice, mineral water, 7-Up and cola. Have enough plain sodas and a few diet drinks on hand for total abstainers. Of course, to be completely covered you would offer rye *and* bourbon, as well as scotch and vodka.

If you already own a set of bar glasses, with different sizes for old-fashioneds (short), highballs (tall), martinis and manhattans (triangle-shaped), use them. But don't *buy* such a set, which is as passé as using ramekins for oyster or appetizer dishes. I vastly prefer using one all-purpose glass for all drinks. It should hold ten ounces of liquid and have a stem. You can buy that glass (made of crystal or glass) at any price.

When serving more than a few cocktails, you'll need more ice than is available from the freezer section of your refrigerator. Order it from the liquor store, but if you have no place to store ice, be sure it doesn't arrive more than two hours before the party. If your party is at seven o'clock in the evening have the liquor/ice delivery at five.

Olives, cocktail onions, lemons and limes can be bought either from the liquor store or at the supermarket when you are getting the food.

Bar napkins (paper is okay here) are good to have; they will save you from circles on your furniture.

# Punches

Sangría, of course, is a kind of punch, and totally appropriate to Mexican and Spanish meals. But generally I don't use or recommend punches; they look too chintzy, as though you're trying to save money. The exceptions would be parties for young people, who are not seasoned drinkers, and Christmas-New Year holiday parties. But it may depend on where you live. We're so sophisticated in L.A., almost to the point of being jaded. You can make a fantastic punch and everybody will taste it once and then head straight for the bar. We once did a party for a group called The Witches and a punch we called Witches' Brew. But it was just a novelty and even the witches had just one cup and that was it. They went for the hard liquor. There may be times when you are trying to create a certain atmosphere that a punch would be all right. But even at those times it's a good idea to be well stocked with hard liquor.

Once I had a great success with a Philadelphia fish house punch at a New Year's Day brunch in Pasadena; the only problem with it was that I got pie-eyed from drinking it and on the way home I thought the freeway was a serpentine. I'll never drink and drive again. Some of the guests went to the Rose Bowl game nearby, others watched it on television sets scattered all over the house, but the brunch—and the punch—went on all day as people drifted in and out.

# PHILADELPHIA FISH HOUSE PUNCH

10-pound block of ice (don't use ice cubes)

6 lemons

4 limes

4 oranges

¼ pound loaf *or* cube sugar (not granulated)

1 cup apricot brandy

1 quart club soda

1 fifth champagne *or* white wine

1 pint 100-proof rum

Start with the block of ice in a large punchbowl about three hours be-fore you plan to serve the punch. Peel the lemons, limes and oranges, and put the peelings in the bowl. Squeeze the fruit into the bowl, mak-ing sure no seeds or pulp go in. Add the sugar (you want it to melt slowly, which is why you use cube or loaf sugar). Add apricot brandy, club soda, and champagne or wine. Stir the mixture about every half hour. Just before serving, add the rum. Makes 40 punch cups.

This is delicious and it doesn't taste potent. But drink just a cou-ple of cups of it and you'll be on your ear. And, with those ingredients, you're not saving any money.

# After-Dinner Drinks

Even in a mundane setting it's always nice to offer liqueurs after a sit-down dinner, although many people won't take them. The most com-mon after-dinner liqueurs (also called cordials) are: brandy, Dram-buie, Cointreau, Grand Marnier, Amaretto, B & B (benedictine and brandy) and crème de menthe. A new favorite of mine is Bailey's Irish cream, kept in the freezer. It's great on ice cream. Because they are all concentrated in sweetness and potency, they are served in relatively tiny portions, over ice or not, usually in smaller (liqueur or cordial) glasses.

The selection of the after-dinner drink is strictly up to the guest and has nothing whatever to do with the meal that went before. If you are going to offer liqueurs it is nice to have a fair selection: get a few bottles and put them on a tray. If you are limiting your selection to one after-dinner drink it will most likely be brandy or its more expensive cousin, cognac. In that case you would simply ask, "Would anyone like some brandy/cognac?"

Cognac is usually more expensive and sweeter than brandy; it has more sugar and is aged longer. While brandy may be made from apples, peaches, apricots, pears, blueberries or cherries, as well as from grapes, true cognac is *always* made from special acid grapes in Charente, a limited district around the town of Cognac, which is 250 miles southwest of Paris. By French law, only cognac produced in this district can carry the word "cognac" alone on its label. Prices of both brandies and cognacs vary widely.

These days after-dinner drinks are usually served right at the dinner table, though occasionally in larger houses the diners will move to another room for coffee and liqueurs. (Europeans do that routinely, but it's now rare in this country, except in certain places, like Pasadena, where there are still drawing rooms. I am always surprised to find that in Pasadena the women still go upstairs to powder their noses, while the men have brandy and cigars.)

I have heard of people drinking pure cream or olive oil before leaving home to line their stomachs, so they can keep on drinking without getting obnoxious. I can't recommend that, but if you do drink too much some evening, have black coffee *and* tomato juice with Tabasco before you go home.

PRECEDING PAGES: *When you've got a big party planned, it is essential to have experienced help. That way you can relax and enjoy yourself along with the guests.*

# HELP!
## When to Hire It

**W**hen you get to the point where you want to have twenty or more people for dinner and you don't want to give them just one quick drink and a buffet-style meal, it's time to consider hiring at least one-in-help. You are still very much in charge of the party, and there is plenty of work for you to do, but a hired maid or bartender can assist you in the serving and cleaning up. Check with employment agencies in your Yellow Pages, not only as to prices but also to be sure that the maid or bartender will provide his or her own uniform and do the cleanup work you require, in addition to serving.

The likeliest one-in-help is the bartender. In addition to setting up the bar and serving drinks (you can now expand your selection of cocktails), the bartender generally tidies up the room and empties the ashtrays. He (or she) can also help you serve dinner; if there is one main dish, the bartender can ladle it out, and the people can help themselves to everything else. Since the bartender can also wash dishes he might be worth the extra expense, particularly if you are alone as host or hostess. If a bartender is good, he can serve from twenty-five to forty people all by himself.

The price will vary from city to city, but you should be able to get a seasoned bartender for about fifty or sixty dollars for the first five hours, and another ten dollars an hour after that. I would suggest staying away from a local college student, unless absolutely no one else is available where you live. The college student will be cheaper, but he will need so much direction that he won't be worth the saving.

A bartender should provide his own uniform: black pants, a white shirt, black tie and a black (preferably tuxedo) jacket.

When deciding to hire a bartender, weigh your needs carefully. Whom have you invited? If they aren't big drinkers, or they all drink the same thing—white wine—a bartender might be a waste. You might then consider hiring a maid instead.

A maid can make a dinner much more elegant. She can pour the wine, clear the table and wash the dishes. With only one-in-help you will still have to pass those pretty platters so everyone is served while it's hot. The maid can place the dessert in the middle of the table, so the guests can help themselves, and you can pass the coffee. There should be no more than ten guests (eight is better) for a sit-down dinner with only one maid, but you can have a full four-course meal, with more than one wine. The maid can also answer the door, hang up coats, keep the ashtrays clean and keep checking the bathroom(s) for neatness. Double-check with the agency beforehand, to make sure that the maid will do all these things, so there are no misunderstandings or disappointments during the party.

A maid is also responsible for her own uniform, which should be a simple black dress and a clean white apron. A cap is optional, but it's correct to ask any help or her agency in advance what she is planning to wear. If you don't like what you hear, buy a maid's uniform that could be used again. If she doesn't like the uniform you provide, she can refuse the job.

It's important that a maid be efficient and unobtrusive; a bartender, after all, is expected to have a little personality of his own, but

*Simple Italian antipasto. Presentation is everything! (top left)*

*A fun centerpiece for a bar mitzvah is made up of baseballs, team pennants in miniature, popcorn and Cracker Jack still in the bags and boxes. (top right)*

*Here's an idea for serving cookies (store-bought or homemade). I've got them flowing in and out of a basket, with a red drum, cinnamon sticks, and apples for a simple but dramatic Christmas sideboard.*

*Red and green napkins in wineglasses scream "Christmas."*

*Only in Los Angeles would an all-pink twilight poolside party look quite like this.*

*These are just a few of the ways to fold napkins in vessels.*

*Mixing different plates (and even glasses) on an old (but clean) quilt, makes a different dinner party for four.*

*My favorite food, a hamburger piled high.*
*Beer makes a nice accompaniment.*

a maid has to carry out your wishes. For this reason it's best to work with an established employment bureau and pay the extra salary involved.

If you have to go to the local diner or restaurant to hire a waitress, be sure to check her out and carefully instruct her beforehand: she shouldn't wear her hair long to serve food; she should put it up first. She should not wear her badge that says "Hi! I'm Gloria!" or "Holiday Inn." Or her usual orange or pink uniform. Make a deal with her to buy a new, conservative uniform, and you may even help her start off in a new business. Above all, she can't be too forward: in restaurants waitresses are used to asserting their own personalities; in your house you should set the tone.

If, after they get to the party, your hired help just doesn't work out, all you can do is fire them—after the party. Bad as they are, it would be disaster to have them leave in the middle of everything. You report them to their agencies (here again, with the college student or the diner counter girl, you're helpless), and make sure the word gets around about about how bad they are.

In my business, maids' and bartenders' uniforms get a little more elaborate than simple black and white, and you may want to think about designing your own for special occasions, particularly if there is a way to use them more than once.

For a Mexican Christmas party I got the women long red and green skirts and very frilly white eyelet blouses and white eyelet aprons tied with a great big bow in the back. A green scarf doubled as a serving napkin for those in red skirts, a red scarf for those in green skirts. The men wore short red jackets, white shirts, black pants, red ties and a little badge saying "Happy Holidays." I used these costumes again during the holidays instead of regular uniforms, making sure the same guests weren't invited.

*A selection of cheese is covered in glass to keep fresh at an outdoor picnic party. (top left)*

*Olives, cheese, breadsticks, fruit, and vegetables combine in a Greek motif. (top right)*

*Fanciful desserts are displayed on a park bench. (bottom left)*

I buy uniforms according to the theme of the party and just charge a small rental fee each time I use them. I keep quite a stock of uniforms at my house, many of which can even be used more than one season. I have Middle Eastern costumes, oriental (which can be made to look Chinese or Japanese), Mexican, Italian, French and, of course, formal. They're all on racks in my garage and we can dress the help up or dress them down.

When we did a calypso party the women were all in peasant skirts and blouses with straw hats. The man were in white pants, bright shirts and frayed straw hats. The guests came dressed in evening wear but we fit into the background atmosphere.

On the day of a party my help all go straight from their homes to the job. If we're going out of town, sometimes we have a meeting place. One person is in charge of the wardrobe and will take it to the location of the party. For a half-million-dollar wedding in Denver the men were fitted with white tie and tails, and the women were in black tuxedos. The wardrobe was all sent ahead from Los Angeles and was waiting in the hotel when we got to Denver. All forty-two of them were responsible for bringing their own uniforms back to Los Angeles. Like everything else in party giving, it's just a question of organization.

# A Word About Being a Good Guest

Good domestic help, as most people know, is getting more and more difficult to find. I think one of the reasons is that people who go to parties are so badly behaved that the domestics take on a poor attitude. Guests need to be educated; some of them are downright rude, I'm sure without meaning to be. A waiter will be passing a tray which requires both hands to hold. Guests will refuse to look up from their conversations, and even when the waiter balances the tray and nudges them on the shoulder they'll ignore him. The waiter will move on to the next person and then the first person will say, "Hey, I didn't get any of that."

Some table manners are just deplorable. Some people will ask for a knife when you serve them soup, simply because they want to see the knife right there in front of them. What are they going to use it for?

The way to be a good guest is to sit tight and see what the hostess has prepared for you. If there's a disaster, go and help her; that's just part of being nice. But asking for catsup before you know what else is coming is just bad manners! It's also bad manners to salt food before you taste it. You'll see plenty of people who will cover food in salt or catsup before tasting it, though the poor woman has knocked herself out preparing it. I once told a man to taste a dish before he salted it but he said no, he knew it was going to need more salt. I was delighted to see that he couldn't eat it. He apologized and had to ask for another plate.

It also isn't right to disrupt service at somebody else's home simply because you want a cup of coffee or whatever else at that moment. Some people are very selfish and will stop a waiter in the middle of serving and say, "Go bring me this." I tell the waiters to hold off until they've finished serving the whole table, then they can get whatever has been requested.

At one of our parties a man stopped every waiter who passed him and asked for a dessert. We met out in the kitchen and there were seven desserts ready to go in to him. We put them all down in front of him and he looked like a fool. We were in a big tent and had to go fifty feet at least to the kitchen to get him dessert, so out of pure orneriness we loaded him up. The people at the table laughed at him, which I hope made an impact on him for the next time. But some people you just can't embarrass nohow.

Remember to respect your hostess' home. Don't badger the hostess or her helpers, and be observant of what she has prepared for you. She should set the pace, and you should watch her to see what she is doing. If you aren't sure what the fish knife is for, wait until she picks up hers. She may even announce that you have to use your knife—to slice a stuffed endive, for example.

# Caterers

If a party you are planning calls for more than two-in-help, you should probably consider a caterer. There are certain times when a caterer is almost always preferable—for your daughter's wedding, for example, when you will have a lot else on your mind and the crowd is likely to be large. You shouldn't hesitate to use a caterer for such an affair if you can afford it, and if the party would be too much for you to plan and carry out.

Check carefully with several caterers in your area (ask other hostesses around town, or look in the Yellow Pages) and get several prices for your proposed party. (In general, a luncheon, or a cocktail party with hors d'oeuvres, will cost somewhat less than a dinner party.) If you find that you'd have to cut too many corners, you'd be better off scaling down the party and the guest list and doing it yourself.

Here are some things you must settle with any caterer before you hire him:

1. Will there be a fee for a consultation or estimate? If so, make sure it is deductible from the cost of the party itself.

2. What is his best-known dish? What would he think of serving to your group? What will be the cost of the food? (Caterers do the shopping; you don't.)

3. Once you've agreed on a menu, leave the preparation to the caterer, but be explicit about what time you want the meal served. What time will he and his crew arrive?

4. Does he provide a bartender? Someone to answer the door? A dishwasher?

5. Are you buying the liquor and wine, or is he? (State liquor laws can be involved here. Sometimes, as a courtesy to regular customers, I order the liquor for them at cost and have it delivered to them.)

6. What is he charging you for the rental of what equipment? (Most people don't realize that caterers have to rent their equipment too.)

7. Who is providing the flowers? At what cost?

8. What is his overall cost *per person?*

Once you come to terms, and the caterer's menu and prices are acceptable, insist on a contract *in writing* to protect yourself. It should include a list of the food and the amounts to be served.

My reputation in Southern California is that of caterer to the stars, or at least to the rich and famous. But there really is no category of party I won't cater. Every year I do a Christmas dinner for two at which I do all the cooking and serving, and I'll also do dozens of parties for several hundred, with forty or more in help. The simplicity or complexity of a party does not bother me—so long as there is a willingness on the part of the host or hostess to spend money. There is a point beyond which you can't cut, and if people do try to cut beyond that point I tell them they don't need me. I would be embarrassed to do it cheaply, and I'm not going to be embarrassed.

If you want a caterer you really have to spend the money. His labor, food and rental costs are what they are, although there can be big differences in the cost of certain items. You and the caterer have to agree on what you want and on how much you're willing to spend for the necessities: chairs, plates, flatware, etc. With new clients, if I didn't make these ground rules clear I could end up giving a free party.

Merely to rent a tent, tables, chairs, glasses and linens for a couple of hundred people can come to more than $7,000. That's without decorations, food and drink.

A caterer is the best judge of how much food to buy. You can save money by serving chicken instead of beef, but don't try to cut the quantities. I've actually had customers who invited a hundred people and bought a hundred shrimp. So I won't let the hostess buy her own food, because the first thing she'd say is that *I* ran out, that *she'd* ordered plenty. I've learned that in that situation a hostess is not going to tell the truth. But I've been known to tell the truth if the guests asked. I'd say very nicely that I didn't know where the shrimp came from because the hostess bought them. I'd serve them just as beautifully, but I wouldn't take the responsibility.

At the lavish Paul McCartney party at the Harold Lloyd estate in 1976, Linda McCartney insisted on having a kettle of her own homemade pea soup. We had built a Mexican village complete with mariachis and street urchins dispensing tacos; we had Nelson Riddle's orchestra playing for dancing at one end of the lawn and a fully equipped disco at the other—each out of earshot of the other; we had three stages for live entertainment, including the cast of *The Wiz* and the Los Angeles Ballet Company. I have never worked so hard in my life! But it was worth all that Mr. McCartney and Wings spent on it.

In the midst of all this activity, there was Linda's pea soup. I was torn between leaving it alone or giving it my interpretation. I doctored it in the end but put a sign on the kettle saying it was Mrs. McCartney's.

One couple I did a party for said they were in the meat business and wanted to provide their own meat. They bought a cut of beef I'd never even seen before. Everything else was lovely, but the guests couldn't eat the meat. I got the blame for it, of course, and afterward I asked them what the hell kind of meat it was. It turned out they weren't even in the meat business, they were just trying to save money. You learn by working, but there are too many nice people to have to put up with much of that aggravation.

A woman called me once to announce that she was going to have the wedding of the year for her daughter. Her budget was $5,000 and she wanted to invite five hundred people. For that you can give them cake and coffee. She didn't want to cut down her list and the $5,000 had to include invitations, flowers and the bride's dress! I talked with her on the telephone and told her where to buy the cake, and otherwise tried to point her in the right direction. I said that with a lovely cake and some sandwiches she wouldn't be able to have too much help, and of course no champagne. She had to rent all the glasses and tables and dishes, and the rental bill alone for five hundred people would have been $3,000. (When she first called me she thought she was going to give them all a sit-down dinner!)

I told her to try to cut down the guest list and to stint on the tables and chairs. Let them stand up. Put the food table in the middle of the room, put all her money on it and make it gorgeous. Have a lovely tablecloth, pretty flowers and monogrammed paper napkins. She wound up with sandwiches, cake and coffee at one end of the table, punch in a rented silver bowl at the other. She used a frozen punch I had recommended, adding ginger ale and ice, and served it with a hulled strawberry in each glass. There is a way you can still make it nice on a limited budget. I understand that the lady followed my instructions and that, if it wasn't exactly the wedding of the year, it was nice.

If you went into a department store and saw a suit that you liked for $200 and you offered the manager $70 for it he would tell you to drop dead or take your business elsewhere; it's the same with catering. My regular customers never ask how much anything's going to cost—except maybe to say, "Don't go crazy on the flowers this time, Milton," or something like that. They buy good food every day and they know what it costs; I don't even have that much of a markup, banking on volume of business rather than on any one individual party.

Once I had an appointment with a prospective client; she asked a lot of questions and wrote down everything I said. She called me back to her house three times, then finally called to say she couldn't afford me. I was annoyed because I'd had her on the appointment book for a four-thirty wedding and had left the afternoon free. So after doing a brunch that same day we were all back at my house drinking some wine. The telephone rang. This same woman was in hysterics. She said, "I used all your ideas and got somebody to do it cheaper, and it's a mess. All the flowers are wilted."

She had an enormous live tree that I was going to loop through with netting and hang with baskets of marguerite daisies. The bridge over the pool was also to be hung with daisies. It was a blistering hot day. The florist had gone there at nine o'clock in the morning and hung the daisies, not in water and not following the shade. Can you imagine? By this time—four o'clock in the afternoon—everything was dead, with half an hour to go before the wedding. She was crying and said, "I will pay you anything to come here and fix things." I said, "You've got a caterer there and I can't come in over that man." But she was crying and said, "You can't leave me like this." So all I did was go over there and pull all of the stuff out of the tree.

The woman was trying to cut corners, and the funny thing is, the person she used instead of me could have pulled it off if he'd had the foresight to keep the flowers out of the sun—just get them ready to hang instead of actually hanging them. I had also suggested that we plant Shasta daisies along the aisle for the bride and groom, and stand there and water them until the wedding began. The other caterer had dug holes and put in daisies, but not in water. On the runner going down the aisle I was going to paint a few little marguerite daisies here and there. He had gone out and bought some wallpaper that didn't even look like daisies, cut out the flowers and stuck them on the runner. It was so tacky. I pulled them off because they looked ridiculous. The woman got what she paid for, but I did feel sorry for her.

People used to do that kind of thing to me quite often: take my ideas and get somebody cheaper to execute them. I had to start saying, "If you're sure you're going to use me, I'll come to the appointment." But if it's just to pick my brains I tell them no. If they give me a deposit (which is against the party, otherwise not refundable) to show they mean well, I'll go. So we've sifted a lot of brain-pickers out. This might be the way your caterer feels also. He may ask for a deposit; and now you know why.

I'm all for keeping costs down, especially if the party's for charity, so long as we know what we're dealing with right from the start. Early in 1980 I catered a benefit sit-down dinner for four hundred on behalf of the Desert Hospital in Palm Springs. We served boned breast of apricot chicken, Chinese peas with toasted sesame seeds and mushrooms, rice pilaf with pine nuts and chestnuts—all on one platter. That way we could have one waiter or waitress for each of forty tables of ten. Ordinarily we'd have had two waiters per table, but cutting out forty in help is a healthy saving. We accomplished it by serving a corn bisque and a hot cheese stick, clearing that off and putting a hot plate down at each place before passing the platter. The rolls were already on the table and cheese and fruit were available on side tables all around the tent.

When you are entertaining at a formal party you would never have the cups and saucers and cream and sugar already on the table—but then you would have two waiters per table. When the party is for charity, and you want to cut costs to increase the cause's proceeds, it is not only acceptable, it is expected that you will cut corners. Guests serve themselves dessert from a buffet table (the best way, in any case, to offer a choice of desserts). Put a pot of coffee or an urn on each table, so that guests can pour their own, and have the cups and saucers, cream and sugar, already out on the table.

Here's an example of what was involved in catering this benefit, which will give you an idea of what a caterer does for any large party.

Equipment:

· 8 butane stoves, with four burners and one oven each, at one end of the tent;
· 2 six-foot charcoal broilers;
· 10 or 12 washtubs and a water hose.

For this party we brought in fresh food from L.A. and the only things we purchased locally in Palm Springs were the butter and cream. Liquor was ordered locally.

For seven o'clock Saturday night the cooks arrived at about twelve noon, organized the groceries, and then started seasoning the chicken. The chicken was broiled on the charcoal first, then it went into pans with a special barbecue sauce. The apricot sauce went on top and then the pan was covered with foil and put in the oven. This was baked so that the apricots plumped up. Then the cooks started the white rice in one big pot and the wild rice in another big pot. Somebody else chopped onions and green peppers and sliced the mushrooms. Everyone was busy. Some of the women came early and made radish roses and cut up celery and carrots.

When my decorators were finished with the top of the tent my tables went in. Ten of the waiters and waitresses kept occupied setting forty tables.

The bartenders arrived at about four, the same time the liquor was delivered. They started setting up the bar, got their lemons and limes out and unloaded the glasses. (Glass boxes are left in a certain area with the silverware and dish boxes on eight or ten eight-foot tables. As these things are washed they can go right back into their boxes.)

I arrived at four o'clock and put the candy and flowers around and checked my tables to make sure they were set correctly. (There's almost always something wrong; for instance, the napkins may not be just right, and I'll fix them. I'll make sure there are matches on all the tables, and cigarettes if we're serving cigarettes.)

The two dishwashers arrived at five o'clock. Whenever a waiter takes a plate into the kitchen he scrapes it and hands it to the dishwasher.

The guests arrived at seven. We had a cocktail area with one big buffet of hors d'oeuvres: peanut butter wontons, gravlax with cream cheese, capers and onions, home-baked pâté, steak tartare, hot guacamole with shrimp and hot corn chips, little spinach and cheese pies, and raw vegetables and dips.

By not having shrimp, lobster or caviar as hors d'oeuvres, and cutting out a few other expensive touches, you can cut catering costs in half. The same party at a hotel would cost somewhat less but not be nearly so nice. Either way, it works out well for the charity, which can charge up to (as in the case of the Republican Eagles at Pickfair) $5,000 a person. With four hundred attending and someone underwriting the cost of catering, the whole $2,000,000 goes to the charity.

For a group that large we cook in washtubs, which fit nicely on four burners. You don't need or want fine cooking equipment for that many people. But whatever the size crowd, I'm a bug on hot things being hot and cold things being cold. I want to stress that this is important for private dinners as well. With just a little organization, your meals can be piping hot for your guests. Heat the platter you'll be passing, just as we do for four hundred, and spoon out the rice and vegetables before you slice the meat.

While our platters are being served, the kitchen prepares for a second passing. As the waiters take the trays back to the kitchen the cooks straighten them out and add more hot food to them.

When the main course is over, we offer cheese and fruit from the buffet. To serve the dessert, which is my favorite part of the meal, we will have laid out all of our dessert plates. Three of the kitchen crew will put the desserts on the plates, then two of us will go around with the hot chocolate sauce, and two more will follow with the strawberries (raspberries in the more expensive version) and the nuts.

Here's the recipe for one of my favorite main dishes; it's perfect for many different party menus.

# APRICOT CHICKEN

Seasoned salt

Pepper

Paprika

½ cup flour

4 chicken breasts, boned and cut in half

½ cup Wesson oil

1 cup barbecue sauce

Mix seasoned salt, pepper and paprika with the flour. Dust chicken with flour mixture and brown quickly in oil on both sides. Remove to baking pan and brush with barbecue sauce. Cover and bake 15 minutes in 400° F. oven.

## SAUCE

¼ pound (1 stick) butter

½ medium-size onion, chopped

¼ green pepper, chopped

2½ ounces canned crushed pineapple

16 dried apricots

½ one-pound jar Saucy Susan or apricot jam

1 cup cooking sherry

In saucepan, melt butter, add the remaining ingredients and simmer for 20 minutes. Add the juices from the baked chicken breasts and spoon sauce over them. Make sure there are 3 or 4 apricot halves on each piece. Cover and heat for 20 minutes at 350° F. Serves 4.

My catering service consists of forty people on the floor, eight in the kitchen, six bartenders and two dishwashers. To get this many for one night I draw first from my regulars and then from my extra list. I've only got five people on full-time salary, but twenty other regulars are able to make a full living working for me if they want to. Many people prefer to be on the extra list because they don't want to work full time. Some have regular daytime jobs and just work with me on weekends, when most of our larger parties take place. I have housewives who enjoy working with me occasionally and are always happy to come when I call. So it's rather easy to get my forty on the floor, so long as I have my basic food crew and my four managers.

If I have to do a second party the same day, I'll take a crew to one and send Gus Myricks, my associate of twenty-eight years, and another crew to the other party. I'll organize the rentals for both.

I teach a lot of my people how to cook; I have them write down my recipes in a notebook so that when I tell them to make persimmon pudding, for example, they know how.

A lot of the people who've worked for me for various periods of time have taken what I've taught them and applied it to their own personal entertaining, upgrading their own standards of living. Because of the exposure to my kind of entertaining they have also become authorities for their friends and neighbors. Sometimes when there's a wedding or a party in their families they'll come to me for advice. Some of the people who used to work for me have their own catering businesses and still ask me to tell them about particular parties that I've given. Some people think I'm crazy to tell them what I'm doing, but I don't care. Let them copy. It keeps me creative.

Rarely is there a Milton Williams party that I never get to, because I do enjoy putting in an appearance. I've had as many as three big parties in one night and made it to all three, although that is tiring. I've even had four in one night, but never five. Actually four was an accident. Somebody had written down the wrong month, but there was no way I could let any of them down.

When I do a party I design the invitations, oversee their printing, and take the guest lists and have the invitations addressed and mailed out from my office. I always ask to see the guest list or to be told who's coming so I don't do the same thing I did at another party they attended. It's necessary for me to remember who was there. I'll have to look it up if it's been five or six years ago, but sometimes the whole thing will come back to me as clear as water, almost every detail. And once I've been to somebody's house I don't have to go back to plan a party. I can do it all over the telephone, which is a big help.

Despite my very detailed memory for places and things, I'm no good at all with names. But I always remember a face. One day I was picking up a flat of raspberries at Farmers' Market in Los Angeles when a woman I'd never seen before asked me if I worked for a caterer. I said yes, I worked for Milton Williams. She said, "Oh, he does all my parties." I said to her and her friend, "Ladies, I want you to know that these raspberries will go to a lovely home for a fabulous party, I'm sure in Beverly Hills, but Milton has just about priced himself completely out of business. I'm surprised you're still using him. But he's a very nice fellow." She said, "When you see Milton tell him hello." I said, "I certainly will."

Gus, who was with me, thought I should have told her who I was. But I didn't want to embarrass the woman since she was lying in front of her friend. If I had said that I was Milton, she probably would have cried, because she was making such a big thing of it. I know the people I work for and I had never seen that woman. But one day I will see her, and she's going to know, and I'm not going to say a thing. I'll just smile.

7

PRECEDING PAGES: *Isn't a wedding the best occasion to have a party? Make use of your beautiful pool, garden, or back yard, if you plan to have the reception at home.*

# OCCASIONS-OR EXCUSES FOR A PARTY

**W**hile I don't think anyone's first few parties should be for a specific occasion, there will come a time when you want to celebrate a particular holiday or someone's birthday. The advantage of giving parties during holidays is that they provide all kinds of possibilities for original food and decorations. For this reason even birthdays and anniversaries are better observed in connection with the closest holiday. Valentine's Day, Washington's Birthday, Easter, Halloween and, above all, Christmas give you the excuse to run riot. Here then, in alphabetical order from anniversaries to Yom Kippur, are the best excuses for a party.

## Anniversary

Some people have their first big anniversary party for their very first anniversary and then continue to have one every year. Some people wait for their fifth anniversary or tenth. And then there are the biggies, like the twenty-fifth and fiftieth. People are often very ticklish about receiving gifts on their wedding anniversaries (except from their spouses) so you can celebrate without asking people to bring gifts. What's really important is asking people to share your happiness on this annual occasion. Since you and your spouse know what you're celebrating, you might want to just have a party and not even mention the anniversary on the invitation. But many of your friends will figure out the occasion, so if you do make mention of it, I think you should stipulate on the invitation "Please, no gifts. Our gift is your presence."

In general, the longer you've been married the more people you'll have at your party. Whether you're giving yourself or someone else a party for any anniversary, it should be done because of the way you feel about the people you know, and not simply as a personal celebration.

Renewing the marriage vows has become a popular feature of anniversary celebrations in the past dozen years or so, possibly coming out of the hippy generation and their philosophy of love, love, love. Also, as more people are living together without being married, those who do get married tend to put more emphasis on anniversaries: it's like getting a medal for lasting.

Helen Reddy and her manager husband Jeff Wald decided to have another marriage ceremony on their tenth anniversary and they asked me to do the party. At the time she was probably the best-known female singer in the world, but my musical tastes are more rooted in the 1940s and 1950s, so I hadn't heard of her. I went out and bought all of her albums so I could honestly tell her that I had them all.

The party had a black and white theme. Expense was no object, so we flew in out-of-season tulips from Holland (it was November), and installed a black and white harlequin tile dance floor. California Governor Jerry Brown performed the ceremony and was the only unmarried person invited among the forty guests. In spite of the formality of the affair, I felt that the wines in the Walds' cellar were too fine to serve to that many people, so we brought in something less extravagant. I also vetoed Jeff's suggestion that a chauffeured limousine be sent to pick up each couple—that would have been a little too gauche. But to make it up to him I had individual wedding cakes for each guest packaged in silver boxes, tied with white ribbon and white roses. A note attached to the box said, "Thank you for sharing this occasion with us." There was one on the seat of each car when the guests left for home.

In 1979 I did a seventieth anniversary party for Anne and Sid Richardson, two friends of mine who were then ninety-three and ninety-seven. He plays golf every day and she walks a mile or two every day. We're already planning another party for their seventy-fifth.

Most of the Richardsons' friends have passed away but they have one daughter, a son-in-law and two granddaughters. Each of the granddaughters brought a friend, and there were twenty-four people that Anne and Sid had met near their home in Laguna Beach, so there were thirty guests. They arrived at six for cocktails and ate dinner at seven-thirty on a Sunday night. Here is the way I handled this party (a modified version should work for any anniversary party for older people):

Because it was in a condominium I set up one big table and put everybody at it. I rented two thrones from a movie property supply house and put "the king" at one end and "the queen" at the other, and the people down the sides. I had little double heart frames containing pictures of the anniversary couple at each place as favors to take home and put on their mantelpieces. Anne and Sid each wore a grosgrain ribbon sash on which I had placed his medals and awards and pictures of their grandchildren.

We brought out little individual tiered anniversary cakes with a few candles on each, a total of seventy. That way, everybody helped blow out the candles, after they sang "Happy Anniversary," because they couldn't have blown out that many themselves. We had two strolling musicians walking around the table playing old songs. Everyone was rocking and singing, yet the youngest people there were the grown granddaughters. Most of the others were in their seventies and eighties.

The cost of the anniversary party broke down as follows: to rent the king and queen thrones was $100. Chairs for the guests were rented for about $5.00 apiece. With the china and glassware, the total rental bill was $600. The live music was $300. The flowers were another $300. The help cost $500 and the food was $35 a person, not that extravagant for a seventieth anniversary. But, by doing much of the work yourself, cutting down the guest list, and borrowing chairs, glassware, tableware and china, you could do the party for less than half that amount. Instead of renting thrones, cover some regal-looking chairs you already own in aluminum foil, or buy two inexpensive wicker peacock chairs at a discount import store. You can use them in your home or sell them with little trouble. The framed favors could be replaced by a simple photocopy of a newspaper front page from the date of the wedding (this also works as an invitation), or give out copies of the couple's wedding picture. The music can be the couple's favorite records, preferably using a tape for convenience in playing.

Not all anniversary parties should be without presents, of course, and the traditional anniversaries lend themselves to certain kinds of presents. The early anniversaries in particular (first, paper; fifth, wood; tenth, tin) suggest imaginative and inexpensive presents and party themes.

A first anniversary party could be all paper—paper plates, cups, hats, decorations. Newspapers or paper bags could be used for the invitations.

A fifth anniversary dinner could be served in wooden bowls and eaten with wooden utensils.

For the tenth anniversary party, deliver invitations that are simply regular soup cans with the label removed and replaced with a new photocopied label giving the particulars of the party. Serve something like beefsteak and kidney pie in a pie tin, and carry out the tin theme in the décor, perhaps by using sardine tins or "tin" foil.

You don't have to stick to the traditional anniversary; don't be afraid to depart from the expected. One of the best twenty-fifth-anniversary parties I ever did was on a Saturday afternoon at the Los Angeles City Produce Market loading docks, which are closed on weekends. The guests met at the couple's apartment and we bussed them down to the docks. Nobody knew where they were going, but we had told them it was to be casual and to dress comfortably. We served Eastern European food to the two hundred and fifty guests from street carts.

Another easy, inexpensive anniversary party idea uses a boxing theme. The invitations are tiny boxing gloves attached to a card;

when I did it, the party was for a twenty-fifth anniversary, so we said, "Please join us for the 25th Round," but you could obviously do it for any anniversary. Serve any food you like, and carry out the theme by using four black aisle standards in a square, looped through with white rope, in the form of a boxing ring. You can do anything you want within that square—have tables for eating, have the dancing there, have a cocktail party inside the ropes, etc. You can use boxing gloves for centerpieces, but otherwise the ring and the invitations really say it all.

# Bar Mitzvah / Bas Mitzvah

When a Jewish boy or girl "becomes a man/woman" the traditional ceremony takes place at a synagogue, with a large buffet feast to follow at the parents' home or in a hotel or club. The food and décor have a tendency to become too standard, almost clichés. But ultimately, the occasion is for the child, and as a caterer I believe in discussing it with the child first, then with his parents. Tell your caterer to zero in on the child's interests and involve him in all aspects of the party. A nice idea would be to have the child write out the invitations in his own hand.

An inexpensive buffet table that is very popular with the thirteen-year-olds is a huge hero sandwich. Have a French or Italian bakery make up a loaf of bread six feet long. Fill it with shredded lettuce, pastrami, kosher salami, beef bologna and mustard, and slice it into large portions.

A bar mitzvah and the party following are attended by people from all generations, but thirteen-year-olds also feel the need to celebrate alone with their friends. One solution is to have a second party that night, without grownups. Rent a jukebox or set up a mini-discotheque.

# Birthday

Adult hobbies and professions can suggest a theme for a birthday party. For someone who likes Broadway show music, give a *Fiddler on the Roof* party. Put the invitations on copies of sheet music from the show, and hire a piano player so the guests can sing show tunes. Have a fiddler playing on the roof as the guests arrive, assuming the party is in a private house. Serve Russian borshch, chicken Kiev *or* brisket of beef *or* stuffed cabbage, and a Russian salad (potatoes, green beans, radishes, celery and onions).

For a man who is in the stock market you can use a ticker-tape décor, with worthless stock certificates or voided checks as invitations. I surprised one man by taking the party to his office; each guest walked in with one bottle or bowl and we took over the conference room. I surprised another with a seven o'clock breakfast party before work. We arrived at five to set up, and cooked hot cakes for forty of his friends.

I think it's always a good idea to have a birthday party in combination with a season like spring or a holiday like Halloween. If the birthday is near Valentine's Day, use a heart theme. If it's in the fall, use Halloween or Thanksgiving decorations. That way, you can take advantage of what's available at that time of year.

A lot of the birthday parties I do are surprise parties. I did a surprise eightieth birthday party for John Factor, the brother of Max Factor. For John's party I had my helpers remove all the pots of plants from his slate terrace on a Sunday morning. When he asked what they were doing they said it had to be washed down with acid, which it does periodically. Then they carried the ovens, the food and the whole party onto the terrace and yelled "Surprise!"

Rella Factor, John's first wife, was really my first showcase. She let me do anything I wanted to. She said she didn't care how much anything cost, that I should just go on and express myself. As a result, her fantasy parties caught on. Not many people would turn a twenty-year-old loose with an unlimited budget, but Rella did.

The first party Rella ever had me do was for Sophie Tucker. I went to the library and got her autobiography, *Some of These Days,* for some ideas. We had pictures on the walls from all Sophie's shows, *Blackface, A Queen and Four Kings,* etc., and I had a woman in blackface going around giving out apples to represent one of Sophie's biggest Broadway roles. People were told to come dressed like Tucker in her feathered headpieces—Sophie herself came in a black wig and nobody recognized her! Among the 375 people attending were a lot of Sophie's old chums from the vaudeville circuit. Jimmy Durante and Jerry Lewis were there (Jerry was the youngest guest). At the time, this was really a feather in my cap. I had worked everything out, from the tents filling the Factor yard to Rella's and her sister Millie's dresses. I had two dresses made to look like fire so the sisters could sing the song "We're the Last of the Red-Hot Mamas" to Sophie. By the end of the evening Sophie was weeping.

A sentimental party for a good friend can be adapted from this concept. Have pictures and mementos from your friend's past hanging on the walls. Or send out a baby picture of the birthday boy as an invitation, and say on it, "Guess who's 40?" Then carry out your theme with pictures from his past.

John's and Rella's thirty-fifth anniversary in 1957 was fantastic. I had tents in the front and the back of the house. Her favorite color was purple, so we did everything in purple orchids and coral-colored camellias, because it was the coral anniversary. The decoration and flower bill alone was $9,800.92, which included satin tablecloths in purple and coral satin, and linen napkins dyed to match for this occasion. When she heard that, Rella told me I'd better talk to her husband. As I started to tell Mr. Factor about the expenses, my voice weakened but all he asked was, "What's the ninety-two cents for?" I said I didn't know. And he said, "If it's going to be gorgeous, go to it." In 1957 that was an astronomical bill for flowers and table coverings, but even though it's a bit more than most of us would spend on a party you wouldn't get very much for that today.

Surprise parties are a special category. They are not for everyone. You not only need to pick the right person for a surprise party, you need to pick the right time. You obviously don't want to upset someone after a stressful day at work, nor do you want to surprise a woman with curlers in her hair. A good time to plan a surprise party is the day someone is returning from a trip and would be glad to see a welcoming group. You are at the mercy of the airline or whatever means of transportation the honoree is riding, but—assuming you have access—you have the house all to yourself to get ready until he or she comes home.

# Christmas

This is perhaps my favorite holiday, because everybody's in a good mood and you can get away with a multitude of things—just keep those candy and nut dishes filled. It's also my busiest season but there are a few parties I do every year. In this season of absolute madness, I may do fifteen parties over a four-day weekend. I cater Danny Thomas' annual Christmas Day dinner in the Arabian dining room I designed for him.

For nine years I've catered—all by myself—an early Christmas dinner for a man and a woman who's not his wife. (That's why they have it a few days *before* Christmas, and at my house.) It's always within a week of Christmas because that also happens to be her birthday. I always keep that night open for them. The party is very romantic and it's been quite a courtship. I serve the dinner myself because they know I will never let their secret out. They always have caviar, and there are six violinists. I give them the china, which is monogrammed, and the glassware and flatware as a gift each year. Now they've got a set of eighteen, so I've had a cabinet made for it.

They give each other incredible presents. Last Christmas he gave her a Rolls-Royce Corniche convertible. I had the car driven up to the front of my house while they were at dinner. It was white and I decorated it with a great big red bow and holly. The chauffeur was dressed like Santa Claus. He carried this huge telegram that I had made, so when he rang the bell and I answered it, I told her she had to sign for it personally. She went to the door and saw the car. On the white glove leather seat was a plaque saying, "I love you," three red roses and a music box playing "Jingle Bells."

For one client who lives in Santa Ana, on the back bay of Newport, we did a Mexican Christmas, right down to the costumes for the host and hostess. I had a red sequined dress made for her and a beautiful red velvet jacket for him. The material for the shirts came from Mexico. (It's fun for me to dress the host and hostess—or the bride—as part of my doing the party. I did the wedding dress for Carla Gettelson, a girl I've known since she was born, matching an eighty-year-old lace veil that had been in her family. I actually went along for all the fittings with her.)

Old-fashioned Christmas parties are my favorites, and I did one last year that comes as close to perfection as anything I've ever done. There were two tables, both covered in bottle-green and red plaid tablecloths. On one were two oil lamps with cinnamon oil set in a nest of holly and surrounded by polished little lady apples, little Seckel pears, nuts and pine cones. On the other table were red carnations, popcorn balls and candy canes. The hors d'oeuvres on the cold table were crab claws and great big shrimp with both a mustard sauce and a red sauce, oysters on the half shell, and a platter of crudités. Hot appetizers included Welsh rabbit with bacon, hot avocado with corn chips and my hot peanut butter sauce with wontons.

There was a choice of three main dishes on the buffet table: beef, chicken or poached salmon. The beef was charcoal-broiled hearts of filet, with a baked crust of mushrooms around it. The chicken was cooked with white grapes, served with semolina with chestnuts, pine nuts and chicken livers. After the guests sat down we served lingonberries, endive and artichoke salad, sweet and sour cucumbers, tiny french-cut green beans with cheese sauce and french fried onions. We offered cheese and fruit and six desserts: hot persimmon pudding, chestnut mousse, an assortment of Christmas cookies, Yule log made with Tobler's fudge, crème brûlée with fresh raspberries and walnut pie.

# Divorce

There's no reason that a couple can't celebrate their separating, if the divorce is reasonably amicable and they can agree on a place. I once did a divorce party for Edward G. Robinson and his wife Gladys. It was really a wake, a last viewing, for their vast collection of paintings just before it was sold. The affair was even televised. The terms of the divorce settlement called for all the art they had collected together to be put up for sale. The paintings were appraised, and prices set on each. If one of the Robinsons wanted to keep a particular painting, he or she had to buy it from the sale.

The party was held at the house they had lived in together, which he kept. Gladys, who was Robinson's wife for thirty years, was a true eccentric. That night she wore a green chiffon dress, green shoes with rhinestones, and a green boa. Suddenly during the party she jumped up on a coffee table, announced that she was the Green Spider and did a dance. Mr. Robinson later married again and built up an even greater art collection.

# Easter

Because the flowers are so beautiful at that time of the year, I really love Easter parties, but I won't do bunny-wabbit-type parties. I've done Greek Easter parties, but even better is a Russian Easter party. You can use eggs decorated like Fabergé eggs as place cards and make the dessert in the shape of large Fabergé eggs. Serve borshch, piroshki, chicken Kiev, and pashka—a real Russian dinner. Have Russian music, violins and a balalaika for atmosphere.

The eggs we use as place cards are expensive, but you can jewel eggs instead of dying them. Go to a notions counter and buy sequins, which you use to spell out the guest's name on the place card. Have little rings of bread with sesame seeds to hold the egg up. Put the bread ring and the jeweled egg on a doily on a plate and make a rose out of the butter. This type of party will be really different because, even though people know a little something about Russia, they don't usually associate it with Easter.

Pashka is very simple but delicious, can be made a day ahead and requires no cooking at all! It's so rich it can serve from 8 to 20.

## PASHKA

  **2 pounds cream cheese (at room temperature)**
  **½ pound butter (melted)**
  **2 cups sifted powdered sugar**
  **3 egg yolks**
  **2 teaspoons vanilla**
  **1 cup blanched, shredded almonds**

Beat the cream cheese at low speed in an electric beater or by hand. Add melted butter and sugar. Add egg yolks, one at a time, and keep mixing. Add vanilla and almonds. Line a large flowerpot or a mold with double layers of cheesecloth that has been soaked in cold water and wrung out. Put in the cheese mixture. Stand flowerpot in a shallow pan and refrigerate overnight. Turn the pashka out on a platter. Remove the cheesecloth. Decorate pashka with colored candies, jelly beans, strawberries or fresh flowers, by simply pressing them onto the pashka. You can even decorate with dyed Easter eggs. I sometimes serve the pashka still in the flowerpot (see photograph in color section), with just the top decorated.

# Groundhog Day

This is an example of taking a holiday and making it your own. Every February 2 we do a party for Ann Rutherford, the actress and wife of William Dozier, the producer. It's her big annual party, and the invitations are giant pictures of groundhogs. She figures everybody else celebrates Christmas and all the other holidays, so she invites people to come celebrate Groundhog Day with her. People clamor to be invited.

# Halloween

This is a party I seldom do, strangely enough. The first thought that would come to most people's minds is a costume party. You have to be very sure of your group to have a costume party (see next chapter).

Last year I got talked into doing a dinner party on Halloween that was also to celebrate a birthday. It was a sit-down dinner but the dress was very casual—no costumes. The first course was an endive and shrimp salad which I served in tiny pumpkins. To do this, clean out the pumpkins thoroughly and put them in the freezer to make them into nice crisp salad bowls. The table looks pretty with a pumpkin at each place. And when the guests lift up the lids of the pumpkins there's the salad. It's delightful. Serve hot cheese sticks with it.

The main course for this party was fried baby duckling. The ducklings were quartered and then fried—but each person was served a whole duckling, four pieces. The guests just picked them up and ate them with their hands, they were so succulent. The duckling was served with hot stuffed brandied peaches, green beans with bean sprouts and Cheddar cheese, and french fried onions.

# St. Patrick's Day

The color green, shamrocks, Irish whiskey and Irish coffee are obvious elements for a party on March 17, but for dinner that night why not have corned beef and cabbage? Make a centerpiece of potatoes and rocks to represent Blarney stones.

# Thanksgiving

For anyone looking for an alternative to the usual turkey dinner, consider the following menu:

### Menu

*Corn bisque, served with cheese sticks*
*Individual stuffed cornish game hens, baked with*
*orange-cranberry glaze (see recipe for glaze in Chapter Fourteen)*
*Orange shells filled with mashed sweet potatoes and pineapple,*
*topped with marshmallows*
*Green beans, with onions mixed in (or fried onions on top)*
*Hot rolls*
*Pumpkin cheesecake*
*Coffee*

A tip for serving vegetarians at Thanksgiving dinner, whatever the menu: keep the gravy on the side, and make extra stuffing that has no meat in it. The vegetarians can make a full meal of stuffing, vegetables, salad and dessert.

Here's the recipe for a delicious pumpkin cheesecake:

# PUMPKIN CHEESECAKE

### CRUST

¾ package zwieback, crushed fine

¼ cup sugar

½ cup melted butter

1 teaspoon cinnamon

Mix together all ingredients and press three fourths of this mixture on the bottom and sides of a 10-inch spring-form pan. Reserve remaining crumbs to use later.

### PUMPKIN CHEESE FILLING

2 pounds cream cheese, softened

½ cup canned pumpkin

½ cup granulated sugar

½ cup brown sugar

1 tablespoon lemon juice

¼ teaspoon allspice

1 teaspoon vanilla

5 eggs, well beaten

In large mixing bowl, beat all ingredients together until well incorporated and smooth. Pour into the crust-lined spring-form pan and bake in a preheated oven at 375° F. for 25 minutes.

## PUMPKIN CHEESECAKE TOPPING

**1 pint sour cream**

**4 tablespoons granulated sugar**

**1 teaspoon vanilla**

Blend all ingredients together and spread over the partially baked cake (after 25 minutes, the cake will not yet be done). Sprinkle with remaining crumbs reserved from crust mixture and bake at 475° F. for 10 minutes.

When cool, place in refrigerator for 5 or more hours. This can be made the day before. Remove from refrigerator 1 hour before serving. Serves 10.

# Valentine's Day

This is an easy one, and basically a "store-bought" holiday, because everything is red (or pink) and white, and heart-shaped—from a heart cut out of ice for a centerpiece to heart-shaped candy and cookies.

Start the meal with half a papaya per person, seeded and filled with canned, fresh or frozen crab meat—served in a heart-shaped bowl or on a heart-shaped doily. Make a little curry sauce for the crab with onion juice, mayonnaise, Worcestershire sauce, lemon juice and curry powder. I don't really have a recipe for it, so experiment with your own proportions. Then carry the heart theme throughout the meal: hearts of celery, hearts of palm, hearts of this and that. Once we had hearts of doughnuts for dessert. Instead of a circle we cut out heart-shaped centers, which we ate hot that night at the party. Then we bagged the ring doughnuts with the heart-shaped holes for the guests to take home for breakfast the next morning to remind them of the party the night before.

# Washington's Birthday

This is also an easy holiday, with cherry pie and paper three-cornered hats and hatchets widely available. I tend to get carried away though. I've flown in cherry blossoms for decorations and I often have a man dressed up as George Washington to serve dessert (which is a variation of cherry pie). Use your imagination—think "American" and have fun.

# Weddings

I've done small and large weddings and I even have one customer I've married five times. She had the same group of people at each of her weddings so I tried to do something different each time. Each of her husbands had died; there wasn't one divorce among them.

The second time around can be as lavish as the first; the bride just shouldn't wear virgin white. I once had a client who wanted to be remarried in white, and I told her that if *she* had the nerve so did I. But I let her know that if anyone asked I was going to tell everybody it was her idea, not mine. I couldn't imagine why she wanted to go down the aisle in a train and all when she'd been married before and had three children. She'd been married to one man for fourteen years, had an ugly divorce, and had gone with her second husband for four years before they got engaged. It just seemed as though the white gown and veil would emphasize her age. Finally, I talked her out of it and we had just as beautiful a wedding. We didn't do it in a church; the minister came to the house. I had her children stand up with her and it was all in good taste. She was very happy afterward but she explained that because she had had such a good time at her first wedding she had wanted to do it just that way again. I reminded her that the good wedding hadn't brought her a good first marriage.

One rule I have when doing weddings is to avoid receiving lines wherever possible. They are tedious. For one wedding I even had it put on the invitation: "There will be no receiving line. Bride and groom will visit each table." If you must have a receiving line, just pass each hand along as you shake it, and be very brief in conversation. Say, "How do you do. How nice to see you," and then look down the line in order to keep things moving, even if there's nobody waiting in line. You can get away with it.

If you have the space at home, you should always entertain there. Even for a wedding there's no comparison. A hotel or a country club is far too impersonal; you may have a private room, but at some point you have to come through the lobby and then everybody else is noseying in. Surprisingly, it is more expensive at home but I think it's well worth it. The difference is the rentals. Given three hundred guests, the rentals would probably cost you $12 per person. But the advantage is that it becomes *your* party, not yours and the hotel's. A hostess is always a better hostess in her own habitat.

When I'm forced to cater a party in a hotel the first thing I do is take over the hotel bathrooms. I put in tampons and Kleenex, fresh flowers and a little sewing kit, and I change that old government toilet paper! I put cologne, aspirin and hand lotion next to the sinks and hire an attendant to be there just to take the edge off. You'd be surprised at the people who notice these extras. They go to lots of affairs but at mine they say, "My God, did you see the ladies' room and all the stuff they've got in there?" Just remember: if you were at home, you'd have these things for your guests, so why not extend the same comforts in any setting? It only makes your affair that much more enjoyable.

All but the very smallest weddings require a caterer; if you opt for a hotel, the hotel *is* the caterer and you have a very limited selection of food. If you must have a wedding reception in a hotel, try to have the option of deviating from their standard menu. If you want to try a reception at home, get hold of a good detailed wedding book well in advance of the date. But I don't recommend your doing it yourself. It's too important a day to mess up.

Hotels and country clubs are usually very sticky about letting an outside caterer in. But I have gained much favor in Los Angeles. I go into a hotel, pick out the menu, decorate the room, do the invitations and serve as a kind of co-ordinator. And I try to get the best meal out of them that I can.

I find I work at the Beverly Hilton quite a lot. For Aretha Franklin's wedding to Glenn Turman the hotel even let me bring in all the food. Aretha was supposed to have had the reception at her home but we had to move it to the Hilton because of the rain. The Beverly Hilton people said they wouldn't have let any other caterer bring the food in but me.

# Yom Kippur

Hanukkah, with its candles and food like latkes (potato pancakes with cinnamon sugar and apples) and brisket of beef sandwiches, and Passover, with its traditional seder, are Jewish holidays more usually associated with parties. But Yom Kippur, the Day of Atonement, is followed by a large though light meal.

I cater one for a woman and thirty-five of her family and close friends every year. They will have fasted for twenty-four hours, from sundown to sundown, so the party is called a break-fast. We start with melon filled with jellied madrilène and caviar, sour cream and chives. A cucumber sandwich goes with that. Then we have duck with fruit sauce, and a dessert soufflé. They don't keep kosher so the dietary restrictions are minimal. Right after dessert they all get up and go home, because it's been a long day.

8

PRECEDING PAGES: *Lotus bowls, chopsticks, and simple flowers provide the setting for an elegant meal of takeout Chinese food.*

# TYPES OF PARTIES

There are several kinds of parties that don't depend on a particular holiday or occasion but can best be described by category. Here they are, alphabetically, from B (bon voyage) to Y (yacht).

## Bon Voyage Parties

This type of party is rarely done nowadays. With charter flights and cheap fares, ocean voyages are not that common any more. But years ago, when it was somewhat unusual to travel abroad, we would do a party using as a theme, say, Maxim's restaurant in Paris or someplace else the person was going to visit. At the Hartfield house on Sunset Boulevard, which Sheik Mohammed al-Fassi bought and infamously redecorated, and where I worked as a busboy and first became a cook, we did a bon voyage party for some people who were sailing on the *Île de France*. It was done in the form of a captain's dinner, with table assignments, the horse races and the music as if we were on board ship.

You could do a bon voyage party for a first trip to Europe or the Orient by taking the theme from one of the countries the guest of honor will visit. This is best done the night before or the day of departure. Little going-away presents, like passport cases and travel diaries, are usually given. And, as a real grabber, send invitations in the form of little suitcases.

# Brunch

This is a good first party. Brunches are usually held late morning or midday Sunday, when most people are available and it need not be in honor of anyone or anything in particular.

Scheduling a brunch is simple—it's always between the hours of breakfast and lunch—which gives it its name—and makes it ideal for weekends since everyone sleeps late after partying the night before. Invitations are handled the same as those for any evening meal. But remember to be specific about the time; it's best to mention that it is a brunch and request an R.S.V.P.

Start with French 75s for a festive cocktail.

## FRENCH 75S

1½ ounces gin or vodka for *each* drink
Juice of half a lemon or half a lime per drink
½ teaspoon powdered sugar per drink
Ice cubes
Champagne

Make 8 drinks at a time in a pitcher or cocktail shaker. Put in gin or vodka for each drink, the lemon or lime juice and powdered sugar. Fill pitcher or shaker with ice cubes and to the top with champagne. Serve straight up, with a twist of lemon peel.

The brunch menu is simple, particularly if you fix your eggs the way I do.

## *Brunch Menu*

*Scrambled eggs à la Milton (recipe follows)*
*Smoked salmon or other smoked fish or ham cooked in vermouth and orange juice*
*Mixed garden salad*
*Fresh fruit*
*Bakery-bought dessert*

## SCRAMBLED EGGS À LA MILTON

Like a soufflé without all the effort and worry.

**3 eggs per person**
**1 prebaked pie shell for every 9 eggs**
**Ragú (or other brand) marinara sauce**
**Grated Jack or Parmesan cheese**

Scramble the eggs *very lightly* and put them wet into a prebaked pie crust. Cover with marinara sauce and sprinkle with grated cheese. Bake in a 400° F. oven until it puffs up—about 10 to 12 minutes.

Other main dishes for brunch include sweetbread and corn custard, creamed chicken and popovers, or spoonbread and fried chicken. Any one of those meat courses is enough for between 12 and 20 people. Serve with cold asparagus vinaigrette, which can be done the night before. Then butter sourdough rolls or bread, sprinkle with garlic and a lot of Parmesan cheese, and broil at the last minute; serve hot.

Cheese blintzes and sour cream, smoked fish, and cheese is another good menu for brunch. With it, or any brunch menu, serve a fresh fruit salad and wine.

At one brunch I took flowerpots and filled them with fudge cake. On top I put jamoca almond fudge ice cream (bought at a local Baskin-Robbins). This is a great-tasting ice cream and I use it constantly. (See the recipe in Chapter Twelve for a marvelous ice cream torte.) Then I covered the whole top of each flowerpot with shaved chocolate to look like dirt. I put one tea rose in each pot, which complemented my centerpiece of tea roses. Then I served the flowerpots in little saucers.

I've since taken the same pots, which are made of clay, and baked brownie pudding right in them. Buy pudding-recipe cake mix and follow package directions, adding a handful of chopped nuts and a teaspoon of instant coffee. To serve, top with shaved nuts and stick a fresh flower in the pudding. Pass a whipped custard sauce. These flowerpots can be baked the night before and then heated up before serving.

# Card Parties

Playing cards and having dinner parties are two very different things, so do them on different nights. If you are *serious* about bridge, poker or gin rummy, plan to serve sandwiches at the card table. There is no point in going to a lot of trouble to prepare food, only to have the cardplayers virtually inhale it in order to get on with their gambling.

Just provide enough sandwiches for everybody, along with potato chips and other snacks, and keep the drinks flowing.

# Children's Parties

The cardinal rule of all children's parties is that each child go home with something in his or her hand. A party favor like a fancy straw or a napkin ring that's really an inexpensive bracelet would make the party last forever.

We usually do children's parties around noon and we generally serve them lunch. The parents drop them off and come back to pick them up later. We then serve the parents hors d'oeuvres and cocktails.

For young children you have to have fairly simple food, like pizza and hot dogs. Other foods children seem to like are drumsticks, spaghetti and carrot sticks. And the best beverage for the party is milk. Think of fun ways to serve the food. Have a New York-style hot dog cart with their choice of toppings or set up the house to look like a real pizza parlor. At one party I served the milk in some little milk bottles, the old-fashioned glass type, with straws.

For the birthday party of the child of a wealthy client we served little filet steaks, chili, tacos and tiny pizzas. We must have had a hundred kids attending, so to keep them all occupied we had a little aquacade and a ferris wheel. There was a hayride, and horses, soda fountain and cotton candy machines.

The invitation was an oversized lollipop, three feet long, tied with a great big bow and hand-delivered. Since they were the swirly kind of lollipops I had the invitations written around in a circle. As the kids came into the party the walkway was lined with even bigger lollipops. It was like something from *Hansel and Gretel*.

Lollipops can also be used as invitations for a more modest children's party; they are colorful, memorable and inexpensive. Instead of an entire midway, a clown or a magician can be hired for a few hours. Again, look in the Yellow Pages. And here is one time when you might profitably check with the local college campus. College drama departments might house some talented magicians, clowns, comedians or whatever. Older brothers and sisters might perform for a modest fee, playing music if not actually doing magic. Another source of a magician or clown might be a local television station. As with a caterer or live musician, agree on price ahead of time, and make sure you know what the magician/clown will and will not do. Puppet shows and pony rides are other possibilities.

All kids like hats, horns and favors. Little girls like to dress up, and if you have a girls-only party let them dress like their mothers, in make-up and high heels. This might work with boys, too; they can wear their fathers' or older brothers' clothes.

A rented jukebox is also a good idea for a child's birthday; you can let the birthday boy/girl pick out the records for it. Or get a live combo of local teen-agers for dancing. Kids from the ages of twelve to fifteen are especially into buying records, so make a record-shaped cake, with little records stuck into the icing.

Another idea is to build a birthday party around a hobby. For a boy who likes baseball, decorate with pennants from the major league teams and have a game of throwing baseballs at milk bottles. Whoever is serving refreshments can wear T-shirts and baseball caps (full baseball uniforms are very costly to rent for some reason).

For a girl who likes horses, build the party around riding. The invitations can be attached to a horseshoe; first-, second- and third-place ribbons can be decorations and place cards; the cocktail napkins can have horses on them; and those serving can wear T-shirts and jockey caps.

# Costume Parties

These are fun if you let the people know in plenty of time to get their costumes. But people, particularly those who go to a lot of parties, sometimes feel the need to outdo each other with their costumes. And other people will have no idea of what to wear, or will feel silly wearing any kind of costume. Many people are not creative, so it's best to know your group and to be pretty sure that they will get into the spirit of a costume party before you try it. I prefer theme parties myself.

One way to make a costume party work is to do *Around the World in Eighty Days,* and have each person come in the native costume of his ancestral country. Your centerpiece can be a large balloon attached with green plant tie sticks to a basketful of flowers. Your food can be from any country in the world (see Chapter Nine), or from several countries.

# Country Fair

This can only be done as a large summertime party. For one fair we did, the invitations went out like a big street bill, and we had banners all across the street announcing the fair. We had a Toonerville Trolley to carry the guests from their cars; and there was livestock, produce, dairy and home economics booths, complete with prize ribbons. In livestock there was the meat; in produce, the vegetables; in dairy, the ice creams and custards; and in home economics the cakes and pies. The country fair idea can be modified, of course, if there is ample lawn space for the guests to wander around. You can have the vegetable, dairy and home economics booths or tables with signs.

I don't approve of so-called "potluck" meals in home entertaining —if *you* are giving a party, *you* provide the food—*always.* But just this once you could make a game of having several people bring their best pies, and giving first-, second- and third-place ribbons at the home economics booth. But you should provide the ice cream to go with the pie.

# Debutante Parties

When you add up all the girls who will be presented at most cotillions (which are held at hotels, usually), their escorts and the chaperones, you've probably got a hundred and fifty people, which is too many to handle for a pre- or post-deb ball party without a caterer.

Each year before Las Madrinas (The Godmothers), the most exclusive debutante ball in Los Angeles, held each year just before Christmas, I give a large party for a client in Pasadena. There's lots of good music. And with the girls in their white formals and their dates in white tie, it's a very pretty, elegant, sophisticated party. The décor for a debutante party comes more from the season—Christmas or late spring in most cases. But otherwise this is just a pretty party to introduce the young ladies to society.

One simple way to entertain a few of the debs and their dates is to hold a midnight breakfast after the ball. Serve chili, or chicken livers and onions in scrambled eggs, with little pig sausages. Or have a honey-baked ham. Serve hot rolls, and tea, coffee or hot chocolate. Also provide fresh fruit and a buffet selection of miniature pecan coffeecakes, which can be store bought.

# Dessert Only

After theater it's especially nice to have people come over for desserts and cheese, or sweet omelets, sweet crêpes and other late night things. Loving desserts as I do, I can go crazy creating things for a dessert-only party. But you can make several desserts the day before or make one thing from scratch and then dress up store-bought goodies. Have people over at nine o'clock just for dessert. They'll love it. See Chapter Twelve for some specific recipes.

# Garden Parties

If you have a beautiful garden you should use it for a party in the summertime, as an alternative to a cocktail party. We do a great many of them but one of my favorites was the one we did for clients who have a big patio off their dining room. We set up one large table with turkey and mushrooms en croûte, pâtés en croûte, and boards of salmon and pâté. There was cold cucumber soup and cheese sticks. Another tea table was set up with desserts, fruits and dessert cheeses. There was a bar at one end of the garden where a lot of the men went. (Some people just cannot be sophisticated nohow!) The women all came in hats, and it was very elegant. The invitation was engraved on écru with peach and silver.

For an English garden party we served ginger cake and Scotch breads from biscuit barrels. A woman played the harp, and a string quartet performed in another section of the garden. For dessert there were fresh strawberries, and orange sections to dip into hot chocolate sauce, while white-gloved waiters went around with bottles of champagne.

Traditional garden parties can be expensive. (See Chapter Fifteen for the budget of the $1,000 garden party for a hundred people.) But it's easy enough to just have a salad party out of doors. There are many low-budget things you can do to make your garden look special for the party. If you have oak trees, or trees that can look like oak, tie yellow ribbons around them. If you have a pool, float candles and flowers in styrofoam on the surface (turn the filter off, to eliminate the noise). Unless you want people to use the pool, surround it with potted plants. If the party is at night, put votive candles between the pots. Hang flowers or lights in the trees, and aim stereo speakers through the windows to provide music. Tie balloons to fences and clothesline hooks (but take the clotheslines down for any party, of course).

# High Tea

This is an English adaptation to use when you have a lot of people to entertain at once, and a rather chic crowd at that. At a high tea there should be enough food to satisfy everybody—those who didn't have lunch and those who aren't going on to dinner. Serve tea at one end of the buffet table and coffee at the other end and a Graves wine on the sideboard. Make sandwiches of olives, cream cheese on date and nut bread, cold rare roast beef and whole wheat bread, cucumbers and smoked salmon or herring with cream cheese, onions and capers. Make the little sandwiches individually or in loaves. To make the loaves, cut the crusts of the bread and slice *horizontally*. Use four slices of bread and three layers of filling. Refrigerate these loaves for a few hours, then slice *vertically* into little sandwiches.

Instead of sandwiches you could do a whole smoked salmon on the table. A carrot, nut, raisin and apple salad is particularly good with the herring sandwiches. Make some tarts to serve as dessert.

Another good dish for high tea is a cold fruit curry over hot rice. Serve it on small plates with more chutney, coconut, chopped peanuts, green onion and chopped bacon.

## COLD FRUIT CURRY OVER HOT RICE

1 fresh mango, peeled and diced

1 cantaloupe, peeled and diced

1 medium-size can pineapple chunks (20-ounce)

1 cup canned or fresh seedless grapes

1 (20-ounce) can pears, sliced

1 (20-ounce) can Elberta peaches, sliced

½ cup raisins

Drain the canned fruits and reserve the juice. Boil raisins in 1 cup of water for 5 minutes and let cool until raisins have soaked up the water. Mix together gently all of the fruit and set aside while making curry sauce. Pour curry sauce over fruit mixture and stir gently. Serve over hot rice.

### CURRY SAUCE

> **2 cups reserved fruit juice**
> **Juice of 1 lime**
> **1 cup chutney, chopped fine (reserve juice)**
> **2 teaspoons curry powder**
> **1 teaspoon chili powder**
> **2 teaspoons cornstarch**
> **¼ cup water**

Boil the fruit juice. Dissolve curry powder, chili powder and cornstarch in water. Add to fruit juice and stir until thickened. Continue to boil for 1 minute. Add chutney. Pour over fruit.

High tea can be from 3:00 P.M. to 7:00 P.M. on a Saturday or Sunday afternoon. It sort of bridges between lunch and dinner. If the guests didn't have lunch they can make up for it, and if they eat enough at tea they won't need dinner. It's a nice alternative to cocktails.

We once really had a high tea: most of the guests kept asking me what a high tea was. I said, "To get high, what did you think it was?" So we served scotch in teacups. Everything was served in a teacup, just like during Prohibition, and it was hilarious. We also served Alice B. Toklas brownies.

We had an elegant table with a lace cloth and a beautiful silver tea service filled with scotch, another with bourbon and another with vodka. I told the hostess to put on a big picture hat and sit there and pour the "tea," very properly, as if she were sucking lemons. It was fun to be there, and the talk of the city the next day. We capitalized on the phrase "high tea," but we had no tea at all—and no coffee either!

# Moving Parties (House Cooling)

A house that is about to be moved out of (or into, if it's in the rough construction or refinishing stages) can be a wonderful locale for a party. The table centerpieces can be paint cans, brushes and electrical wiring, and the waiters can wear construction uniforms. The invitations might be building permits or fake leases. And instead of chairs, have your guests sit on packing crates. Have the wine chilling in garbage cans. If the walls are going to be repainted anyway, let your guests write a fond farewell or a welcome-to-the-neighborhood note on them. Then take pictures of the wall for your album.

I did a moving party for the Henry Mancinis that had a band playing inside a moving truck parked in the driveway. The food was barbecue style and it was a lot of fun.

If it's feasible, have before and after parties; the before being the house cooling, the after being the housewarming in your new home.

# Office Parties

Most of the office parties I do are for people whose parties I also cater at home. I'm asked to do things like the opening of a stock exchange. But these parties are mostly boring. Often people who hire me for a party in the home use a more conventional caterer for office openings. However, one Los Angeles paper magnate throws a hell of a party in his office building every five years. Five years ago we handled a thousand people a day for four days running.

I did another party to open a block-long office building in the Westwood section of Los Angeles, using a third of the lobby for an octagon-shaped dance floor, a platform for the orchestra and a sweet table. The 325 guests were invited for five-thirty in the afternoon, but many of them stayed until after midnight. Trelliswork with burlap behind it and about a hundred yards of material tented the lobby to warm it up. Seven large poles covered in brown fabric held up the tenting. I made the poles into oak trees by wiring on huge branches of real oak leaves that were turning autumn colors, which I had flown in from Baltimore. The poles really looked like trees. I scattered some more oak leaves around the floor and a janitor came around and started raking them up. I said, "Would you please put those leaves back," and he said, "It looks terrible." I said, "That's the way I want it." A wooden fence, marvelous sheaves of corn stalks, and huge white lanterns hanging under the harvest moon completed the décor.

We were planning to do a ground breaking for that same building in early 1978, but it rained so hard that season that the big tent and scaffolding we were going to put up wouldn't stick in the leveled ground. We were going to have a big scoop shovel crane packed with ice and champagne bottles. The invitations were already out in the form of a real shovel, but we got rained out. The earth was so soft that we couldn't put the heavy equipment or the scaffolding, which was going to be a buffet, on it. My little brain child got rained on. But it would be a great opening for somebody someday on a construction site.

A farewell party for a fellow worker is the simplest and most frequent kind of office party. This is a situation in which you might be splitting expenses among several people (unless the company is picking up the cost), and a potluck selection of hors d'oeuvres could conceivably work out, so long as you don't have several people bringing the same thing. If there is no refrigeration available, use washtubs for the wine and the ice, and have an expert-amateur from the office staff volunteer to be bartender. The theme of the party can be either bon voyage (if he or she is going a distance away), or centered around the new job, or possibly the guest of honor's hobby—in a retirement or leave-of-absence situation.

# Progressive Dinners

I think these really work only in small towns. A different person is responsible for each course and the guests move from house to house. We do parties at which the guests all go to one person's house, where they are put on a bus and nobody knows where they're going. The bus will stop somewhere and you've got hors d'oeuvres and drinks already set up. Then you put them back on the bus and take them to another house where you've got a dinner all set up. You get them back on the bus and take them for dessert, liqueurs and coffee at still another house. We've done that a lot, but only with one person or one couple acting as host and paying for the whole thing.

# Yacht Parties

It's kind of hard to do a party on a boat because they don't really have kitchen facilities. But it can be worked out. We did a birthday party on a yacht that just stayed in the harbor. We had twenty-seven people and a pirate party theme, with gangplanks. It was very cute. I'd much prefer to do the whole party on the dock next to the boat. There are disadvantages to entertaining on boats, like slippery decks. At one party I did for seventy people on a huge yacht out of Wilmington, California, a woman fell and broke her wrist. I'd never say no to the challenge but if I had my choice I'd forget yacht parties and do a party on a huge ocean liner instead.

PRECEDING PAGES: *Takeout chicken and these ingredients make an easy chicken paprikash (see page 8 for recipe).*

# ECONOMICAL ETHNIC EATING

Some national cuisines are more imaginative than others, like the Chinese and French—which are also more familiar, thanks to a wide variety of restaurants devoted to them. But any ethnic tradition, from American Indian to Czechoslovakian, can provide a dinner party that is colorful, original and economical. My own favorites are Italian, Rumanian and Hungarian (which are almost alike), Spanish, Mexican and Greek.

## Italian

For Italian parties, why not make your own pasta and cook it right in front of the people? We used to roll it by hand, but now there are electric pasta-making machines that produce any form of pasta in four minutes—without kneading. Put up string for the pasta to dry on. If there isn't room for everyone to watch in your kitchen, do the drying in another room. Have pots of water boiling to cook the pasta, and three or four different sauces simmering in full view of the guests. It's very showy.

It isn't hard to make your own pasta—just flour, water, oil and egg. If you don't have the electric machine the rolling is the hard part. You can make green pasta with spinach and orange pasta with carrots. Carrot fettuccine is delicious. Fettuccine, linguine, spaghettini, rigatoni, macaroni, etc., are just names of the different sizes of noodle. The same pasta maker produces them all. The electric one is a little noisy, but it goes very quickly.

As an entertaining gimmick and part of showing off as a chef, it's nice for people who are really into it to be able to say, "I make my own pasta." But for most people I wouldn't recommend making your own except for this party idea; it's a lot of trouble and neither cheaper nor better than store-bought. Unless the making of the pasta is part of the party, buy it.

I make many different kinds of spaghetti sauce, but if you start with just the basic one you can add anything you want to it. I love spaghetti or linguine with clam sauce. You can make a red clam sauce by adding to the basic sauce recipe.

## MILTON'S BASIC SPAGHETTI SAUCE WITH CLAMS

**2 cloves garlic**

**1 medium-size onion, chopped**

**½ green pepper, chopped**

**3 tablespoons olive oil**

**2 (28-ounce) cans tomato purée**

**½ cup red wine**

**1 teaspoon orégano**

**Coarsely ground red pepper**

**Salt to taste**

**2 (7½-ounce) cans minced clams, with juice**

**2 (10½-ounce) cans whole clams, with juice**

Sauté the garlic, onion and green pepper in olive oil, add the tomato purée, red wine, orégano, red pepper and salt to taste. Cook down for 12 minutes, then add the clams. Cover and let simmer about 20 minutes. Serves 8.

Alternative additions to the basic sauce instead of clams would be:

1. Two pounds of mild Italian sausage, sautéed; each piece of sausage should be cut into five segments.
2. A vegetarian sauce can be made by substituting 16 medium-size mushrooms, sliced and sautéed, for the clams.
3. Another meatless version is made with one large eggplant (peeled or not), diced and sautéed.

If you're not making fresh pasta for your party and you use store-bought, cook the pasta according to package directions, or test for the firmness you want, and bring it right to the table in a big pot—after draining the water off, of course. Give your guests a choice of their favorite sauce. When I cook pasta I add one tablespoon of chicken stock base to the water (use real chicken stock if you happen to have it around); you can eat it that way without sauce, it's so good.

With a salad, lots of Italian bread, fruit and cheese, a store-bought Italian dessert like spumoni, and one Italian wine (white or red, depending on the sauces), you have a lavish and still inexpensive dinner.

An elegant Italian appetizer whenever fresh artichokes are available is stuffed artichokes al pesto.

# STUFFED ARTICHOKES AL PESTO

**6 young baby artichokes**
**Salt**
**1 egg**
**Ground pepper**
**4 teaspoons grated Parmesan cheese**
**⅔ cup dried mozzarella cheese**
**½ package Armanino Farms dried pesto sauce**
**2 or 3 sprigs chopped fresh parsley**
**½ cup dried bread crumbs**
**5 tablespoons olive oil**

Discard outer leaves of artichokes and cut off stalks at the base. Pull leaves apart and sprinkle with salt. Beat the egg, add a pinch of salt, freshly ground pepper, cheeses, pesto mix and parsley. Mix well and stuff this mixture between the leaves of the artichokes. Sprinkle with bread crumbs. Arrange the artichokes in a large wide baking dish or casserole, spaced well apart. Sprinkle with olive oil and add a few tablespoons of warm water at bottom of dish. Cover and bake at 375° F. for 25 minutes. Uncover and bake 15 minutes more, until brown. Salt and pepper to taste. Serves 6.

For an Italian Sunday brunch, offer one of two main courses, veal Florentine or fettuccine. Both are simple to make.

# VEAL FLORENTINE

12 slices veal leg (have the butcher cut it)

1 pound pork sausage

1 medium-size onion, chopped

½ small green pepper, diced

Olive oil for sautéeing and browning

1 (10-ounce) package chopped spinach, defrosted and drained

Salt and pepper to taste

4 eggs, beaten

Seasoned bread crumbs

Cheese sauce (recipe follows)

Pound the slices of veal to flatten them. Sauté the sausage, onion and pepper in olive oil. Add the spinach and salt and pepper to taste. Spread this mixture on the veal slices; fold over and roll the veal. Dip each slice in the beaten eggs, then roll it in seasoned bread crumbs. Dip in the egg again, and roll in the bread crumbs again. Then set aside rolled-up slices to dry, about 10 minutes. Brown the veal in olive oil quickly. Put veal in a flat pan and heat for 15 minutes in a preheated 350° F. oven. This can be made the night before, or early in the morning, and heated just before serving. Serve with cheese sauce. Serves 8, 1½ veal rolls per person.

## CHEESE SAUCE

16 mushrooms, sliced

4 tablespoons butter

2 (10½-ounce) cans Aunt Penny's (or any other brand) white sauce

½ cup Italian dry white wine

½ pound grated Swiss or mozzarella cheese

Dash of Tabasco

Sauté the mushrooms in butter and combine with remaining ingredients in a saucepan. Heat and serve over the rolled-up veal.

# FETTUCCINE

**2 pounds white fettuccine**
**3 teaspoons chicken stock base**
**1 tablespoon olive oil**

Cook fettuccine according to the directions on the package, omitting the salt and adding the chicken stock base and olive oil. Drain and toss with sauce while the noodles are still hot.

## SAUCE

**1 pound butter**
**1 cup grated Parmesan cheese**
**1 cup (½ pound) ricotta cheese**
**1 teaspoon chopped chives**
**1 teaspoon chopped basil**
**1 cup heavy cream**
**½ teaspoon chicken stock base**

In a saucepan melt butter, add the Parmesan cheese and stir constantly over medium-high heat until the cheese is melted. Add the remaining ingredients, blending well.

This entire dish takes approximately 20 minutes. While the noodles are boiling, the sauce is being made.

Serve either the fettuccine or the veal—or both—with fresh Italian bread, soft butter, Gorgonzola cheese, a white Italian wine (like a Soave) and a big Italian salad.

# Rumanian (Hungarian)

Every so often my clients who are also my friends will cook for me, and I enjoy nothing more than an Eastern European dinner made by one of them. Margot Factor was born in Rumania; her father was Hungarian and her mother was Viennese. Like all of those people from the old Austro-Hungarian Empire, Margot can really cook. She's taught me everything I know about Rumanian, Hungarian and what she calls "Near Eastern boundary food."

Margot's specialty when it comes to main courses is duck and fried sauerkraut. Rumanian, Czech or Hungarian duck is distinguished from other duck (such as the French duck à l'orange) by being cooked very, very crisp with no glaze or sauce at all, just the natural gravy. Besides the delicious fried cabbage, other accompaniments to a Rumanian/Czech/Hungarian duck dinner would be potato purée, a cucumber salad and crème caramel for dessert. While there is some French and Italian influence evident in Rumanian cuisine (Rumania was the resort area of the eastern Roman Empire, hence the name, and Rumanian is a romance language), all three countries offer basically peasant fare, which is filling, festive and frugal.

## MARGOT FACTOR'S FRIED SAUERKRAUT

Drippings from cooked duck
1 medium-size onion per can of sauerkraut, sliced very thin
1 or more (27-ounce) cans Libby sauerkraut
Salt and coarsely ground pepper to taste
Pinch of sugar

Put the drippings from the cooked duck into a skillet and brown the onions in them. Rinse and squeeze out the saukerkraut and add to the fat and onions. Add salt, pepper and a pinch of sugar (I add a pinch of garlic but Margot doesn't). Continue to fry until the sauerkraut is *almost* brown.

The Hungarians and the Rumanians serve a kind of antipasto, a group of appetizers which I like so much I use them as hors d'oeuvres for other kinds of parties as well. The platter consists of: white caviar, cold peppers and eggplants, cheese and mateitei, which is a Rumanian sausage that's made up fresh by Roshoff's Delicatessen in Los Angeles (and, I'm sure, by other stores in other cities).

White caviar is made with carp eggs and onion juice which are beat up into a substance like mayonnaise. You then add olive oil very slowly as you continue beating. With just a little salt and pepper, it's very tasty. Both the eggplants (figure one for every four persons as an hors d'oeuvre) and the peppers—red and green—have their outer shells burned over a gas flame and then peeled off. Cut both the eggplant and the peppers in pieces, add oil, lemon juice, a little garlic, salt and pepper. (The peppers also get sprinkled with vinegar.) Both are served cold. The mateitei, Rumanian in origin but also served in Hungary, are cooked over charcoal.

While Rumania and Hungary, along with Russia, Poland and Czechoslovakia, have similar first courses, like piroshki (yeast dough filled with meat, then fried or baked), each country has a few that are unique—Hungary's goulash soup, for example, or Rumania's meat salad, which is made of cold diced leftover roast (any kind), peas, carrots, peppers, mayonnaise, lemon juice and marjoram.

Chicken paprikash is perhaps the most famous Hungarian main dish, and you can serve the simple recipe from Chapter One, or you can make it from scratch, with spätzle which are little Hungarian pasta shells. Paprikash salad is made with cucumbers seeded and sliced the long way, and white onions and cooked celery root which you then marinate in an Italian dressing. Hungarians also delight in puff pastries, not unlike Austrian, but those you can buy from the nearest Austro-Hungarian bakery.

*All the ingredients for the perfect pork roast.* (*Chapter 15, page 206*)

FOLLOWING PAGES: *I designed and decorated this kitchen for a Los Angeles client. Here it's set up for a Christmas buffet served right from the kitchen.*

# Spanish (Mexican)

Spain's food is far more delicate and subtle than that of Mexico, which is hot and spicy. But since Americans rarely eat anything as fiery as the Mexicans do at home, and since both cuisines depend heavily on chicken, fish and rice, we can put the two together for our party purposes.

Paella, the best-known dish from Spain, is not so cheap any more because the price of seafood has risen quite a bit, along with its consumption. But our budget-conscious party givers can substitute arroz con pollo (chicken with rice) for paella by adding little bay shrimp to it. If you want to add a vegetable dish, have a pisto, which is just onions, tomatoes, green peppers and zucchini, all diced, and cooked with olive oil and salt and pepper. You can serve that hot or cold.

## ARROZ CON POLLO (WITH SHRIMP)

1 frying chicken, cut in eighths
Seasoned salt, pepper, paprika, flour
¾ cup olive oil or vegetable oil
1 large onion, sliced
½ green pepper, diced
8 mushrooms, sliced
1 No. 2 can solid pack tomatoes
3 (10½-ounce) cans chicken consommé
2 tablespoons Worcestershire sauce
1 (16-ounce) can pitted black olives
16 large peeled and deveined raw shrimp
2 cups uncooked rice
Pinch of saffron
Chopped green onion
Sliced pimientos
½ cup grated Jack cheese

*Geese are the main dish for this Christmas dinner, but any meat or fowl would look just as good surrounded by poached peaches filled with cranberries, holly, poinsettias, cheese, fruit, and breadsticks.*

Season fryer with seasoned salt, pepper and paprika and dust very lightly with flour. Heat oil over high heat and brown chicken quickly. Remove chicken from pan. In same remaining fat, sauté the onion, pepper and mushrooms. Return chicken to fat and stir together. Add tomatoes, consommé, Worcestershire sauce and olives; salt to taste. Cover and simmer for 20 minutes. Add shrimp, rice and saffron. Give a stir and cover tightly again. Simmer for another 35 to 40 minutes, shaking pot occasionally. Garnish with green onion, pimientos and cheese. Serves 4.

An easy and cheap appetizer for a Mexican or Spanish meal is empanadas. The simple way to make them is with Pillsbury Crescent Dinner Rolls from the dairy case. Roll a piece of Jack cheese and a piece of jalapeño pepper (canned or jarred) in each crescent. Bake according to the instructions on the package and serve them hot. They're delicious and taste like you baked 'em yourself!

Follow the empanadas with arroz con pollo, or try the even cheaper potato tortilla. Both go well with pisto. Serves 4.

## POTATO TORTILLA

**8 red or 4 russet potatoes, sliced thin**
**Salt and pepper to taste**
**Olive oil**
**8 eggs, beaten**

Salt and pepper the potato slices and cook them in a little preheated olive oil. Keep stirring the potatoes until they begin to clarify—at least 10 minutes. Pour the excess olive oil off the potatoes and set it aside. Add the potatoes to the bowl of beaten eggs. Clean the skillet, use the reserved olive oil and add some fresh oil to it. Pour the egg and potato mixture into the skillet after the oil is hot again. Keep pushing the potatoes and eggs around until they are completely cooked on one side; the eggs will get thick on the bottom but still be wet on top. Lift the half-cooked tortilla out of the skillet onto an oiled plate. Turn it over and slip it back into the pan to cook the other side. When it is brown on both sides take it out and cut it in wedges like a pie. Serves 8.

Place pitchers of white or red sangría along the table. Use different-colored napkins and mix-and-match plates. Serve slices of green pepper and other raw vegetables on plates decorated with parsley. Provide several wheels of cheese and crackers or bread. Cheap and simple as it is, it's a gourmet Spanish/Mexican dinner. Add a piñata and green and red crepe paper streamers from the dime store to one of these two Spanish meals and you have a Mexican Christmas party.

# Greek

A slightly more involved (and expensive) Greek meal than the buffet we described in Chapter Two would feature—in addition to moussaka —roast lamb with lemon and dill, which I happen to love. We did it as part of an authentic Greek dinner for Janice Taper, a long-time customer of mine and a well-known Los Angeles socialite and patron of the arts. Her father is Mark Taper, founder of a large savings and loan association, for whom the Mark Taper Forum is named.

Janice has a house that was recently done over as a lady's pad in Trousdale Estates. It's all done in shades of apricot, and she has a lot of fabulous Chinese porcelains, Japanese lacquer boxes and French Regency furniture. It's put together so well it looks just like art. To celebrate Janice's new house we did another party that featured foods from all over the world, using many of the recipes in this book. There is nothing more festive than a national menu in combination with an occasion like a housewarming or a holiday.

Here is one of my favorite Greek recipes:

## ROAST LAMB WITH LEMON AND DILL

**8-pound leg of lamb (have butcher butterfly it)**
**Black pepper**
**2 teaspoons dried dill weed**
**Seasoned salt**
**Juice of 1 lemon**
**1½ teaspoons dried onions**
**1½ teaspoons dried celery**
**Paprika**
**2 tablespoons olive oil**
**½ cup dry sauterne**
**½ lemon**

Season the inside (lean) part of the lamb by rubbing with pepper, 1½ teaspoons of the dill weed, seasoned salt and lemon juice. Sprinkle with onions and celery. Roll up the lamb, fat side out, and skewer at bottom or tie with twine. Put in baking pan and season top and sides with seasoned salt, paprika, pepper and remaining ½ teaspoon dill weed. Rub well with olive oil. Pour sauterne into pan. Bake in a 400° F. preheated oven for 20 minutes, lower heat, basting two or three times during cooking. If you like lamb pink, cook straight through at 400° for 30 minutes; well done, cook for 40 minutes. When done, squeeze ½ lemon over the top. Serves 8 to 10.

# American Indian

All ethnic cuisines are not necessarily from other countries, even if they are foreign to someone's particular experience. I've never been to New Orleans but Cajun cooking is special in this country, and has contributed to the cooking style of black people all over America; the gumbos we make in Los Angeles have roots in Louisiana. American cooking of all kinds has made a big comeback.

For some regular clients of mine who go to every party in town and give several big ones each year in their huge back yards, I did an American Indian party. I put up teepees and had smoke coming out of several of them. We did authentic American Indian food: a lot of peanuts and berries, fried cornmeal mush with chicken, and dried beef with sweet butter on whole-grain bread. That menu and concept could easily be scaled down to a smaller back yard, budget and guest list. Have just one teepee, rented or bought from a camping goods store, and have a fire going in front of it. If you have any hired help they can wear Indian head bands to serve in. Feathers can be used in many ways for decorating and for dress.

# Scottish

We had this party two years after the Indian party, for the same people, to outdo ourselves. (But this too can be scaled down.)

A Loch Ness monster rose up out of the swimming pool. There were bagpipes, and dancers doing the Highland fling. We had putting greens, because golf is very big in Scotland, where it was invented: and a hammer and gong to test your strength, which they also love up there. We also had archery available. Needless to say, we used up the whole property.

At the front of the house I had a scenic designer do a thirteen-foot-high castle set. As you drove into the driveway there was a moat with water in it and a bridge over it. There were knights in armor who introduced the guests as they came in. Waiters and waitresses wore different Scotch plaids and shields. They served Scotch breads, barley soup and other foods from Scotland. All drinks were poured into pewter tankards—including scotch.

You can use this theme by getting Scotch plaid tablecloths, and perhaps even asking your guests to wear tartan skirts and clan ties. Serve a barley soup, mutton stew and Scotch shortbread. Decorate with small pots of heather and play music from *Brigadoon*.

# Southern American

In spite of my roots, I'm not at all crazy about the idea of putting a chitterling in my mouth, and the only way I like grits are in a grits soufflé. But it's hard to ignore the revival of interest in Southern cooking, and it can make an easy, colorful and inexpensive dinner party. Get bottles of pancake syrup shaped like Aunt Jemima or Mrs. Butterworth (full or empty) and tie the details of the invitation to the bottle. Hand-deliver them. Or get the art class in the local high school to design a Southern motif for your invitations and mail them. You can also buy little cotton bales (I once sent away to New Orleans for some to use as invitations), which would also make a nice table decoration. The meal—which could be brunch or supper—consists of fried chicken or ham, grits soufflé and apples fried in butter and brown sugar.

## GRITS SOUFFLÉ

8 eggs, separated

4 cups cooked grits (see package for directions)

1 pound sharp Cheddar cheese, grated

2 cups white sauce (homemade or canned)

Dash of Tabasco

2 tablespoons grated onion

Salt to taste

¼ pound (1 stick) butter, melted

Beat egg yolks and egg whites separately. Combine all ingredients except egg whites. Fold in egg whites. Pour into a 2-quart buttered soufflé dish. Bake for 1 hour at 375° F. Serves 8.

# Chinese

There is no simple way to fix good Chinese food at home, unless you want to take a course in wok cooking. Find a good Chinese restaurant and order dishes (even days ahead) to take out the night of your party. Serve the meal in inexpensive lotus plates you can buy at a discount store, and provide chopsticks. Decorate simply, with three or five carnations or other flowers, in oriental vases. For dessert serve canned lichee nuts, canned mandarin oranges or canned white peaches, on a bed of ice. And, of course, fortune cookies, which are more fun than they are tasty.

PRECEDING PAGES: *A healthy salad can be a meal in itself for the dieting guest. Chock the bowl full of fresh vegetables and the salad will be as lovely to look at as it is to eat.*

# SALADS:
# A Must for Every Meal

I think every meal has to have a salad. It adds a freshness to the meal. A salad can be anything from a simple lettuce, tomato and onion salad to a whole endive stuffed with egg, capers and toasted pecans. Both of those ideally take a homemade vinaigrette dressing and are served on chilled plates with chilled salad forks.

You can appropriately serve a salad four ways: as a first course; with a meal; after the main course; and there are fruit salads for dessert (I hate fruit salad as a first course). But *never* serve two salads at the same meal.

Here are three examples using salads before, after and during a meal:

## Salad Before

Peel and hollow out a small tomato for each person. Fill the tomato with egg salad, turn it upside down on a bed of limestone lettuce. Cover with bottled Thousand Island dressing augmented with bits of fresh seafood. Serve before any main course except seafood.

# Salad After

After a main course of beef, chicken, lamb or pork (again, not fish or seafood), serve mixed lettuce and other greens, tossed lightly with oil, vinegar and herbs and chunks of a ripe cheese (like Roquefort). Serve with a sesame cracker dipped in butter and heated.

# During the Main Course

With lamb stew and wild rice, have a Caesar salad sitting on the table. With that kind of meal you need fresh greens right along with the meat.

For your Mexican or Spanish meal, make your salad with sour cream, avocado and grated Jack cheese. It could never be bad. Shred lettuce, add oil, vinegar and pepper, then sour cream, jalapeño peppers and diced avocado. Toss that all together and add pitted black olives if you want to. If you flake tuna over all of that, it is fabulous.

An Italian salad to accompany a meal has more in it than most. Cut up hearts of romaine lettuce, radishes, celery, green peppers, black olives, cucumbers, cherry tomatoes, red onions, artichoke hearts and fried red peppers. Add bits of fresh dill and fresh basil, crumbled feta cheese and hard-boiled eggs, boneless skinned sardines and prosciutto diced very fine.

# Salad Bar

What's fun to do in the summertime in the evening is to have a whole table full of salads. Take all the salad greens you can get—spinach, lettuce, watercress, etc.—and put them into a great big bowl. Then have plates of cut-up roast beef, breast of chicken, fresh shrimp, bacon, ham, Swiss cheese, Jack cheese, Cheddar cheese, olives, artichokes, radishes, chives, fresh herbs and green onions. You put it all out like a smorgasbord. The guests go around the table and make their own salads, and you give them a choice of dressings. Serve a lot of hot bread, and with wine and dessert this meal is really quite hearty.

I could eat three or four plates of that do-it-yourself salad and not want for anything else. You can also do an Italian variation of it, with salami, pepperoni, avocados, olives and cherry tomatoes. I've even had it with herring or other pickled fish. You can also try it with fruit of various kinds and cottage cheese.

We've done this salad bar for everything from bar mitzvahs to beach parties. The table is gorgeous and you let your guests serve themselves on big plates. We put signs on each of six or seven dressings to let people know what's in them, and have a dish of fresh crumbled Roquefort cheese. Once we covered a table with lettuce leaves on a sheet of mylar. On top of the lettuce leaves we alternated crystal bowls and wooden bowls with all of the ingredients. To make the table look even prettier we put bunches of scrubbed radishes and whole artichokes between the bowls.

11

PRECEDING PAGES: *Fresh vegetables create a refreshing array of colors when displayed imaginatively in matching coffee jars without their labels.*

# DIETARY RESTRICTIONS

If you cater to everybody's whim, you may have twenty-five different dietary requests for your two burners and one oven. There are people who will actually impose on you to that degree if you allow them to. You have to be cordial to people when they are in your home, but if you unknowingly serve them something they just don't happen to eat, it's not your fault. It is always a good idea to have a grapefruit or any piece of fresh fruit—a melon if it's in season—in the house to offer someone who refuses dessert for whatever reason. A good host or hostess should try to be aware of the ongoing dietary restrictions of the people on the guest list. And a good guest should let you know his or her needs ahead of time.

## Salt-Free Meals

If I know in advance that someone on a salt-free diet (increasingly common today with so many open-heart surgeries) is coming to dinner, I will cook something special for him. It is easy enough to cut out the salt by making a portion of whatever you are serving in a separate little pan. Your guest will appreciate your thoughtfulness, and the evening will be more enjoyable for everybody. You shouldn't overly salt things, anyway, since you can always add salt but you can't take it away.

# Kosher Meals

To be completely safe, it is advisable to serve your kosher guests a dairy, vegetarian or fish meal, eliminating meat entirely. The reason for this is that the guidelines for the purchase and preparation of kosher meat may prove difficult to follow if you are not already familiar with them. But if you do choose to serve a meat meal, be aware that meat and poultry must be purchased from a kosher butcher (where non-kosher meats, such as pork, are not sold). Also, no dairy product may be used in the preparation of, or served with, any of the components of the meat meal. So, for example, you must use non-dairy margarine for vegetables and non-dairy creamer for coffee if you are serving meat.

A large variety of fish, which need no special preparation (and can be bought anywhere), can be served to guests who keep kosher. The only category which is completely out is shellfish.

As for serving dairy products (except with the meat meal) and vegetables—usually anything goes. Sometimes those who keep kosher prefer to eat only those hard cheeses which bear the certification "kosher" on the labels. If you wish, ask your guest about his or her preference.

Be sure, when shopping, to read the ingredients on labels in order to watch for lard or animal shortening in pastry products and beef stock in canned soups.

If you plan to serve wine, buy a kosher brand.

Don't worry about serving on your dishes; if your guest has any reservations about using dishes which have served non-kosher meals, it is safe to assume that he or she will mention this to you.

These are some basic guidelines. I have completed a full course in kosher dietary restrictions, but you won't be expected to know everything. Your guests will appreciate your thoughtfulness and will enjoy themselves even more because of it.

In large gatherings there will always be a few kosher guests, so I always make a few kosher dinners. Here's a good, uncomplicated menu:

### Kosher Menu

*Tomato soup or* pure *vegetable soup (no meat or meat stock)*
*Fish with any sauce*
*Salad (no meat products or shellfish)*
*Cake and ice cream*

# Vegetarian Meals

Vegetarianism is more and more prevalent these days. At a large gathering we usually have enough fresh vegetables and fruit available to accommodate our vegetarian guests. They will also eat nuts. If you know that one of your guests is a vegetarian it's a simple enough solution to make an extra amount of vegetables! Try a menu of stuffed mushrooms with walnuts, cauliflower with cheese sauce, fresh green beans, salad, cheese and fresh fruit.

The Maharajah of Mysore is a vegetarian only two days a week, but when he came to Los Angeles, I was asked to do a party for him on one of those two days. I had to come up with a vegetarian meal. I made up a main course of small red potatoes, chives, peppers, onions, water chestnuts, peas, carrots, wax beans, Belgian endive and artichokes in a vegetable potpourri with a dill and olive dressing, similar to a heated potato salad. The Maharajah loved it, and I've used the recipe since.

# Dinners for Dieters

People who are weight-conscious will often do little things during the meal so that they will enjoy themselves without worry; for example, they'll cut out the bread or the starches in a meal so that they can have some of the dessert. Actors particularly figure the extra pound won't show up on them right away if they are filming the next day. But they do discipline themselves more than most people. On the other hand, with some people you can nail their feet down and pour pure cream down their throats, and they wouldn't gain an ounce. I'm so envious of them because if I merely look at something fattening I gain weight.

For a group of people who are all watching their weight you can put out a lot of raw vegetables, with or without a packaged dip, and they can always nosh on those. But you would have to have an awful lot of dieting people at your party to make them a special salad dressing or other slimming dishes. It's just not fair of them to expect you to do that for them. Your facilities are limited and if your guests are that serious about their diets, they should eat at home and come to the party later for the company. The thing that always kills me about many people who say they are dieting is that they will sit down, eat the soufflé with sour cream, take butter and bread, ask for the extra sauces on whatever—and demand Sweet 'n Low for their coffee!

No one would hire me to do a party for dieters and I happen to think it's a terrible idea to have one. Dieting is individual, and the responsibility for losing weight lies with the individual. I'm very conscious, having a bit of a weight problem myself, of what puts on the pounds, so I don't oversalt things, nor do I use MSG (monosodium glutamate) in cooking. Both salt and MSG lead to water retention. But knowing how I believe in desserts (see next chapter), no one goes to a Milton Williams party to lose weight.

With all the diet books on the market and restaurants offering meals that go along with the Pritikin and Scarsdale diets, your friends should be educated enough about their diets to pick and choose from among what you are offering.

I will share one of my own diet meals (low calorie *and* salt free) but, again, one that I think is better pursued in the privacy of your own home and weight-losing program, not at someone else's party:

## 250-CALORIE FILLET OF SOLE FOR ONE

Put a 6-ounce piece of fillet of sole in a Teflon pan; cover with shredded lettuce and season with dried dill, dried Italian herb seasoning and black pepper. Cover and cook for 7 minutes, without turning. Since there is no oil or butter in the dish it is only 250 calories. If your diet can handle more than that, add half a cantaloupe or some strawberries for dessert.

Don't worry too much about it because today the trend is toward simply eating smaller portions, so you can go to a big party and eat a little bit of what most appeals to you.

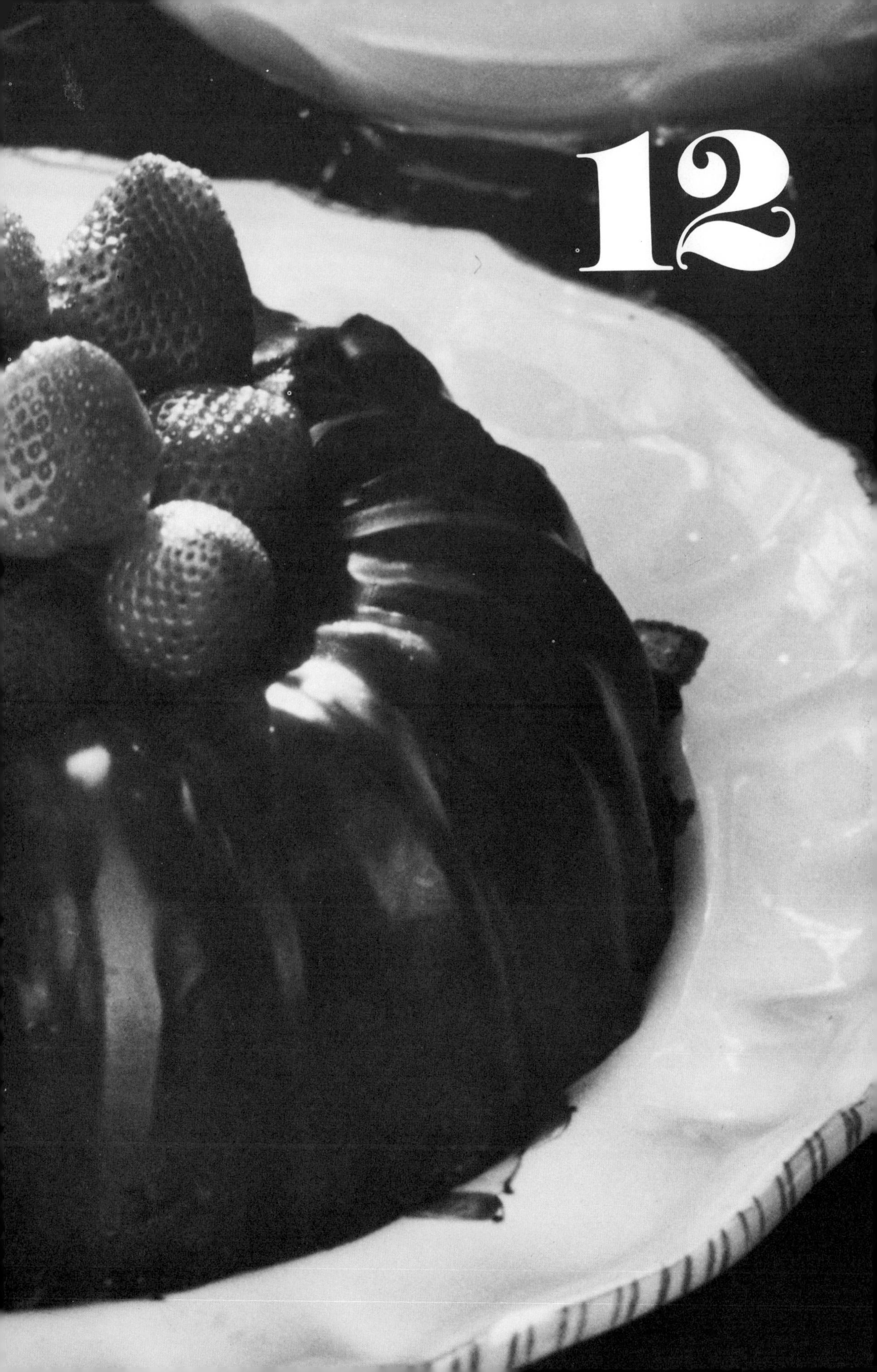

# 12

PRECEDING PAGES: *Fondue Au Chocolate will satisfy even the worst chocolate addict. It is so rich and wonderful, your guests will be begging for the recipe (see page 177).*

# DESSERTS:
## Finish with Flair

**D**esserts are my favorite part of any meal, but that isn't the only reason that they rate a chapter of their own. Desserts are the finale, and therefore the most important impression made by any dinner (or lunch). So, even if the rest of the meal has been simple, the dessert should really flip your guests out, and leave them wanting to come back to your house for more. Better yet, serve more than one dessert—like fruit and cheese, plus a sweet dish—and really dazzle 'em. I always serve something that has chocolate in it, which I've found over the years is almost everybody's favorite.

None of this means that you have to spend a great deal of effort on the desserts. In fact, throughout this book we almost always recommend buying your desserts already made to cut both costs and preparation time. But you can still make a big deal out of store-bought sweets. As with everything else in party giving, *presentation* counts most. Once, with some nervousness, I cooked an elegant formal dinner for a French gourmet society which had been founded back in the thirteenth century. The members raved about the whole meal, but the thing they remarked on most was a very simple water ice I had concocted from bottles of Rose's lime juice. For dessert at a lunch I catered in honor of the First Lady of the Ivory Coast we simply served New Zealand strawberries (ours were out of season)—and champagne.

People love ice cream, and there are many simple yet marvelous things you can do with it ahead of time. Start with the best store-bought ice cream you can afford and make a fabulous ice cream torte that can be frozen a week before your party.

## ICE CREAM TORTE

2 sticks (½ pound) butter

1½ cups cake flour

2 teaspoons vanilla

1¼ packages lady fingers (16) split in half

1¼ quarts each Baskin-Robbins jamoca almond fudge ice cream and any
   French vanilla ice cream

½ cup pecans

1 (3½-ounce) can dry, shredded coconut, toasted

36 strawberries

1 (10-ounce) can Hershey's chocolate syrup

Mix butter, flour and vanilla into a crust and place in a 12-inch spring-form pan. Bake in a 350° F. oven for 15 minutes. Line the baked crust with the split lady fingers; stand them up, baked side out. Then alternate the two ice creams in alternate layers. Add pecans and toasted coconut. Wrap in foil and freeze. Just before serving, decorate with fresh strawberries and ladle on chocolate sauce. Serves 18.

Figs and crème fraîche are a little more complicated, but delicious, and something your guests won't get everywhere they go. Peel the figs and make your own crème fraîche to pour over them.

## CRÈME FRAÎCHE

½ pint sour cream
1 pint whipping cream, whipped
½ teaspoon lemon juice
½ teaspoon sifted powdered sugar

Fold the sour cream into the whipped cream and add lemon juice and powdered sugar. It must sit at least 24 hours before you use it. If you don't use it all, save it, as it makes a kind of culture. Keep adding to it and you have this nice thick cream with the taste of pure cream all the time.

Desserts with fruit are always appealing. You can make apple charlotte using Comstock (or any canned) pie apples. Arrange the apples on a baked pastry shell. Caramelize ½ cup sugar, add 1 tablespoon butter, a pinch each of cinnamon and lemon rind, then pour this glaze over the apples so that it makes a crusty shell. It is very simple, and it would be a waste of time to do the apples and crust from scratch.

When blueberries are in season, make a simple and delicious blueberry pie or individual tarts using this basic crust recipe.

## BASIC CRUST AND LINING FOR PIE

2 (8-ounce) packages cream cheese
1 tablespoon powdered sugar
½ teaspoon vanilla
¼ pound (1 stick) sweet butter
1 tablespoon powdered sugar
1½ cups cake flour
½ teaspoon vanilla

Combine first three ingredients and beat them together very well; set aside. Take butter and remaining ingredients and crumble together by hand to make a piecrust like soft cookie dough. Flute the dough into a pie plate or individual tart dishes. Bake the crust at 350° F. until brown. Spread the cream cheese mixture on the bottom of the crust.

## BLUEBERRY FILLING

1 (8-ounce) jar currant jelly
½ smallest can frozen orange juice concentrate
2 (1-pint) boxes fresh blueberries, washed and drained
Lemon or lime juice
Cool Whip or whipped cream

Heat currant jelly and orange juice concentrate together until melted, and pour over the blueberries. Put the blueberry mixture on top of the cream cheese mixture in pastry shells and refrigerate. Just before serving, sprinkle a little lemon or lime juice on top of tarts to bring out the flavor, and top with whipped cream or Cool Whip. Serves 8.

For picnics, have individual tarts using the same crust recipe. At a buffet, have a basket of the baked pastry shells and bowls of strawberries, raspberries and blueberries, each covered with the currant and orange sauce. And in another bowl have the cream cheese mixture. If you want to go beyond those three choices, add banana cream, coconut cream and cut-up peaches. Make up the tarts upon request. This presentation makes a beautiful dessert cart, and everybody gets to make his or her own pies. Have a bowl of ice cream balls to make the pies à la mode.

You could carry out the same idea more simply with a cart of just ice cream balls and a selection of do-it-yourself sundae toppings. It looks just fabulous as you wheel it around the table and makes a fantastic impact as a dessert. Men particularly love it.

There are two very easy cakes you can create that will make an impression on your guests way beyond the effort involved. The first is a cheesecake using the pashka recipe from the Easter section in Chapter Seven. Simply eliminate the almonds and put the mixture into a store-bought graham cracker crust. Decorate with fresh fruit.

The second is this delicious sunshine cake. Both can be prepared the day before your party and refrigerated.

## SUNSHINE CAKE

2 (8-ounce) packages Nestlé chocolate chips
1 pint whipping cream, whipped
1 pound English toffee candy, crushed
1 store-bought lemon or orange sponge or angel food cake cut in four
   sections *horizontally*

Melt chocolate in a double boiler, then cool slightly. Fold in whipped cream. Cover the bottom layer of the cake with one layer of chocolate cream mixture and one layer of toffee. Repeat with two more layers of each. Ice with remaining chocolate mixture. Serve with your favorite chocolate sauce for a really rich and memorable dessert. Serves 6 to 8.

My dear friend Joan Borinstein is an excellent dessert cook and often does dessert-only parties. She did an all-chocolate party in honor of Maida Heatter's *Book of Great Chocolate Desserts*. Joanie makes two of my favorite desserts and I couldn't choose between them, so here they both are:

# CELESTIAL FRUIT

4 peaches—all kinds
4 plums—all kinds
1 nectarine
1 large mango
1 large papaya
Strawberries
Sugar
Grand Marnier or Triple Sec
½ pound bittersweet chocolate
4 cups whipping cream, whipped
Champagne grapes

Peel and slice all fruit into thick slices (plums don't have to be peeled). Arrange fruit—only *heavy* fruit, save berries—in layers in Pyrex dish. Sprinkle each layer with sugar and liqueur and marinate overnight.

### ASSEMBLY

1. When ready to assemble, melt chocolate and allow to cool. Use fine imported brand of chocolate.
2. One hour before serving, drain fruit so no liquid remains on slices. Place a layer of assorted fruit in bottom of glass serving bowl.
3. Add layer of whipped cream, then drizzle ribbons of chocolate on top (honeycomb-like). Continue with layers to the top of bowl.
4. Do not put chocolate on top. Decorate top with rosettes of whipped cream and insert strawberries and sprays of champagne grapes. Serves 8.

# FROZEN CHOCOLATE MOUSSE

Can be frozen up to two weeks ahead.

# CHOCOLATE COOKIE CRUMB CRUST

**8 ounces chocolate wafer cookies (sometimes called icebox cookies)**
**3 ounces (¾ stick) sweet (unsalted) butter**

Adjust rack one third up from the bottom of the oven and preheat oven to 375° F. Separate the bottom from the sides of a 9 × 3-inch spring-form pan; butter the sides only, then replace the bottom in the pan and set aside.

Crumble the cookies coarsely and crush them in a food processor or blender (or place them in a plastic bag and pound or roll them with a rolling pin) to make fine crumbs; you should have 2 cups of crumbs. Place them in a mixing bowl. Melt the butter in a saucepan and stir it into the crumbs until thoroughly distributed. Pour about two thirds of the mixture into the prepared pan.

To form a thin layer of crumbs on the sides of the pan: tilt the pan at about a 45-degree angle and, with your fingertips, press a layer of the crumbs against the sides, pressing from the bottom up toward the top of the pan and rotating the pan gradually as you press on the crumbs. They should reach the top of the pan all the way around. Then place the pan upright on its bottom; pour in the remaining crumbs and, with your fingertips, distribute them over the bottom of the pan to cover it. Press them firmly to make a compact layer.

Bake for 7 to 8 minutes, remove from oven, cool completely.

# MOUSSE

**1 tablespoon dry instant coffee**
**½ cup boiling water**
**1¼ cups granulated sugar**
**12 ounces semi-sweet chocolate**
**4 extra large eggs, separated**
**3 cups whipping cream**
**Pinch of salt**
**⅛ teaspoon cream of tartar**

Dissolve coffee in water in heavy 2-quart saucepan. Add ½ cup of the sugar and stir over moderate heat to dissolve. Adjust heat to low. Add chocolate and stir until melted and smooth. Add egg yolks, one at a time. Set aside to cool completely.

In a large bowl, whip the cream until very stiff. In a small bowl, beat the egg whites until foaming; add salt and cream of tartar, and continue to beat until the whites hold shape. Gradually add the reserved ¾ cup of sugar, one large spoonful at a time. Beat until the meringue is firm. Gradually fold chocolate mixture into the whites, then fold the chocolate and egg white mixture into the whipped cream. Pour into the crumb crust, smooth the top, or form swirling pattern. Place mousse in freezer. After an hour, cover the top with airtight plastic wrap. Freeze overnight or for up to two weeks.

To remove from pan, use a sharp, heavy knife for cutting around the sides of the crust, and remove sides of pan. Now use firm, wide metal spatula: insert spatula gently under crust, ease it around to release the dessert completely from the bottom of the pan. Return to freezer until serving time. Serves 6.

*A great hors d'oeuvre is cocktail franks arranged around a Sterno can covered with parsley and red cabbage. Guests cook their own, so the franks are always hot. (top left)*

*Pomegranates and persimmons in a Chinese bowl make a simple, effective buffet decoration. (top right)*

*Jumbo shrimp cocktail surrounded by ripe pears and holly makes a lovely and delicious appetizer.*

THE PARTY BOOK

*Hermine Weinberg's 40th birthday party (see Chapter 15). The birthday was hers, the fantasy mine.*

*A section of the buffet table at Marisa Berenson's wedding—incorporating a piece of art, an idea that can be adapted by anyone.*

*The after-dinner table at Helen Reddy's anniversary party: cheese, liqueurs, and coffee things.*

One of my most delicious chocolate desserts is *fondue au chocolate*. It can add elegance to any dinner—but beware, your guests may not remember the meal after they've sunk their teeth into this. Here is the recipe, and there is a photograph of it at the beginning of this chapter. This should be prepared the night before your party.

## FONDUE AU CHOCOLATE

**12 squares semi-sweet chocolate**
**¼ pound (1 stick) butter**
**1 tablespoon vanilla extract**
**18 eggs, separated**
**½ cup sugar**
**Strawberries (or other fruit in season)**
**Heavy cream for whipping**

Melt chocolate and butter in double boiler with vanilla. In a separate bowl beat egg yolks and sugar until a light lemon color, about 4 or 5 minutes. Slowly pour melted chocolate mixture in with the egg yolks. Stir until well blended. Beat 12 egg whites until they form soft peaks; fold into chocolate mixture until well blended (you can freeze remaining egg whites in ice cube trays and use later). Pour mixture into well-buttered bunt mold. Refrigerate for 18 hours. Unmold on platter and fill center with berries. Serve cold with whipped cream. Serves 12.

*Milton's own Christmas table, with a single pine cone and pear at each place. The caviar is optional.*

**13**

PRECEDING PAGES: *The best way to handle any disaster is to stay calm and improvise!*

# DISASTERS

A disaster is only a disaster if you let it get you down. There is absolutely no way for me to anticipate your particular disaster—I have enough trouble trying to anticipate my own. But I know that there are only two things you can do about a disaster: (1) you can pass out; or (2) you can have courage and *do* something about it. Perhaps by recounting a few of my worst disasters I can inspire you to be cheerful in dealing with your own as they occur.

You *can* turn disaster into victory. Once we were making chateaubriand out of New York stripper. To make it you take four big hunks out of the whole stripper, broil it on four sides and cut it on the diagonal. I cut into the first one, then into another, and it was all well done. There was no medium—much less rare. It looked as if we were going to have to serve baked steak. I sautéed some green peppers and onions real quick, and put in some Campbell's tomato soup, wine and herbs. I sliced the meat down—thank God, it was tender—and covered it up so that nobody could ask for rare.

It looked as if it was supposed to be done that way, and my salvation was that we could call it chateaubriand au poivre vert. The hostess said, "I've never had pepper steak this way." I said, "What kind of pepper steak did you think I was talking about?" They loved it so much that every time we go there to cater a dinner we serve the same steak. I do it with fettuccine now and sometimes I do it with spinach.

Spanish turkey is a dish I invented back at the beginning of my career when I only had one-in-help. I had told the client she could buy the main course, anything she wanted, and I would cook it when I got there, an hour or so before dinner. I got to her house and she'd bought a 28-pound turkey! So I cut each leg in three pieces, and the breast into quarters, dipped it in Bisquick and milk and tried to fry it. While it got brown in the frying pan, it still wasn't done. When I bit into it, it was just as if I had fried a biscuit or a doughnut around it. Inside the turkey was still raw, so I had to steam it. I gave the guests an extra forty-five minutes for drinks and hors d'oeuvres. When I steamed it the turkey got done but it had all this brown crust mixed up in it, so I covered it over with a sauce of Spanish olives, tomatoes from cans I found in her cupboard. It was beautiful when we put it on the table. I served it in a big collar of rice with chopped pimientos and chopped parsley. The dish looked fabulous and it tasted good. We've kept Spanish turkey in the repertoire. The key to success in both these cases was not to panic and to deal with what I had. Instead of totally changing the menu, I reworked the food available. This is how new recipes are discovered. In a real pinch, takeout food that's served imaginatively will have to suffice.

There may be many times when you serve something different from what you started out to cook. Another example of this was when I served crème brûlée. It's supposed to be solidified. You bake it slowly in water and it becomes like velvet. Then you chill it and sprinkle sugar over it. You put it under the broiler and it makes a kind of sugar shell. This one time something went wrong and it just didn't work; the crème brûlée was just all lumpy. So I took vanilla ice cream and mixed it in, browned some sugar and pecans in a skillet real quick and poured it on top. I put the whole mess in big wineglasses and threw a big strawberry on the top of each. I took it into the dining room and the hostess said, "I've never had crème brûlée served this way." I just smiled and said, "Something different."

Never admit that anything went wrong until it's all over. A confident attitude will pull you through the worst disaster. I remember the chocolate soufflé that ended up being a chocolate soufflop. It didn't come up. I quickly made some zabaglione sauce and put it on top of the chocolate, and added some crushed English toffee candy that happened to be in the kitchen cupboard. I called it hot chocolate toffee pudding. I later found out what had happened to the soufflé. My crew had forgotten to fold the egg whites into it.

You can almost always go through a cupboard and find something with which to save the day. But for the ice cream for the crème brûlée we did have to run out quickly to the store. Once I saw the dessert wasn't going to work, I told the crew to slow that table down.

Don't assume you are stuck in the kitchen when disaster strikes; you may have to run next door or to the store for something that will save the day. Just draw out the courses to stall for time. If dessert is the disaster, serve coffee first. Pass those candy dishes. And don't be afraid to pull out some ice cream you have stocked, just in case the dessert can't be salvaged at all.

At one big dinner party we had a disaster with dessert and I told the hostess I'd decided we were going to let the guests' stomachs rest. I would give them some coffee now and serve dessert in the living room in a little while. She said, "What a clever idea." It wasn't a clever idea at all. I was stalling. I told the waiters to "crumb" the table, empty ashtrays—very slowly—and start to serve coffee. We brought out the liqueurs, along with some chocolate and other candies. (Another good reason to *always* have candy.) We served all of that while we were trying to rescue dessert, and they loved it. Some people even copied that! For me it was simply survival, while everyone else thought it was chic.

We had a birthday party for a man whose wife bought her own cake, a fragile sheet cake. They liked to gamble and it had poker chips and little tiny cards stuck in the icing. One of my crew lit the candles and picked up the cake, then suddenly dropped it on his way into the dining room—how, I will never know.

People were sitting out there at that dining-room table waiting for the cake and ready to sing "Happy Birthday." I told the waiter to go in and give them some coffee and the champagne they were to have had with dessert. The people waited and waited while we started picking up this cake, chocolate and marshmallow icing, and fishing through it for the cards and poker chips. I saved all the chocolate I could and put it on a board. I put a layer of ice cream on it, then beat up some egg whites and sugar to make a meringue-like topping in the shape of a beehive. I told one of my crew to wash off some of the cards and chips. I put the meringue in the oven and turned it up to broil. Immediately after I took it out, we stuck the little playing cards into the meringue and I flamed some sugar cubes and stuck them on there. Because I don't play cards, I didn't know how to put the poker hand back in the right combinaton, but the dessert still made a statement.

Just as I was telling my assistant to go into the dining room and sing "Happy Birthday" the hostess burst into the kitchen, her voice trembling. She demanded, "Where's my cake?" He said, "This is it." When she asked what happened to the cake, I told her that we had picked it up and the whole thing fell apart. She said, "I knew there was something wrong with that cake when I bought it." I'm sure that baker caught hell, and I'm sorry. It tasted good, and the toasted coconut I put on the ice cream made the meringue stick. All of a sudden out of nowhere and out of necessity had come this dessert, and we got through the party.

One of the worst times I ever had in anyone's kitchen was when a newly wedded bride locked me in her closet before her husband came home because she wanted him to think that she had done all the cooking. She just opened the cupboard door and told me to go in there. I had no idea why. It was a big walk-in closet and she locked the door behind me. At first I just thought it was strange; I tried the knob and I was locked in, but I didn't make any noise because I knew she must have had a good reason for what she was doing. Later, when she finally came to get me, I was really angry. After I found out what she was up to I went along with her little game. I never told the husband. But I never understood why she hadn't just asked me to come earlier to cook the food and leave it for her to heat up.

Over the course of twenty-eight years in business I've had some unpleasant things happen. The wedding cake that fell in the pool was bad enough, but once there was a man who did a flamenco dance and sat down at the piano bench, only to fall over dead. Nobody could eat the food. The host said to me, "Well, he couldn't have died from your food, he didn't get any." The funny thing was the dead man hadn't even been supposed to be invited to the party. The host had run into him at the Farmers' Market, found out the man was going to Argentina for Christmas and said insincerely, "That's too bad, because I'm having this party and I would've invited you." The man changed his plans to fly to Argentina the day after the party. So he went to the party unwanted, did his dance, and died. I don't mean to sound flippant. It was really very sad. But it is an occurrence you cannot anticipate.

Sometimes disaster strikes across the continent and I have to fly in to rescue a party. One of the worst of those times was at a special gallery in Washington, D.C. The party was in honor of California artists. It wasn't really my party and I was only there as a favor to a friend. To give it a very "California" feeling I had brought chili and confetti rice on the plane with me. I ordered Mexican cookies and orange sherbet to be delivered locally. The committee was supposed to have handled the tables, chairs, the serving logistics and décor.

We couldn't start setting up until four-thirty in the afternoon when the gallery closed, and everything had to be ready by seven.

When I got there they had two six-foot buffet tables for a hundred and fifty people, and they were lost in this great big foyer. And they were actually going to pass the sangría! They had some pieces of blue felt they were going to pleat and thumbtack around the tables. When the flowers arrived, they were wilted; it was embarrassing. I told the ladies to set up another separate five-foot table for the sangría and glasses while I went out to get some more flowers.

It had started to rain and I couldn't get a cab to go to Pier One in Georgetown. When I finally got one, I was so drenched I went back to the hotel to change, and paid the taxi driver to stay with me. As we went to Pier One we passed a little flower shop. I could see through the window a woman who had some zinnias, iris, marigolds and pyracantha in little cans. I stopped the cab, ran into the shop and told the woman I was a caterer from California doing a party at an art gallery. I showed her the only I.D. I had, which was my checkbook, and told her to call the gallery to make sure I was legitimate.

After she did I said, "Can I have you, and all these flowers?" I told her that she could cut the flowers off the plants and keep the growing part; she should close the store and take the flowers to the gallery, while I went on to Pier One to look for vases. She looked at me and said, "Okay," and started loading her station wagon. We met back at the gallery. I had bought candles, clay pots, some big Mexican glasses and some tall vases. I also bought a crate of limes, and it is like the war debt buying limes back there. I told the man I wanted the whole crate from his store, and he said they were forty-nine cents apiece. I said I didn't care, I needed the whole crate. He said, "What am I going to do for limes?" I said, "You're going to sell them anyway, aren't you?" Disgusted, he said, "Well, I've got to count all those limes." He started counting but finally gave up and just estimated the number. I stopped at a fabric shop to buy fabric and pins, then at another shop for lanterns.

When I got back we completely covered a thirty-foot-long buffet table and it looked fantastic when we got through. We had fifteen tables of ten set up for the guests to eat at. There was a piñata on each table in the shape of a bull, with little flowers stuck on toothpicks on the back. I ripped those out, cut big holes in the backs of the bulls and stuffed them full of iris and other flowers I had gotten from the woman. After I showed the women how to fold the napkins I went out and got five cases of California wines. It was tricky icing the wine, since it was a California dinner and I wanted all the labels to show.

I managed to finish everything right at seven o'clock and was ready to leave. Not knowing who the guests were going to be, I was surprised when Mayor Bradley of Los Angeles came in. We chatted awhile, and then Vice-President Mondale and Senator Kennedy arrived. I was very glad I had gone to the rescue. I went back to my hotel and by ten o'clock I was on the plane to Los Angeles; I had a huge party here the next morning.

Although this was a very large-scale party, the one aspect that you can apply to your own disaster is to get help. Pull your best friends over and tell them what has happened. They can help set up, serve or entertain if you have to slip out for a little while.

When I entertain at my house I don't expect disasters, even

though my parties are usually spontaneous. Somebody will come into town whom I want to see and I have to make the time. But on one occasion I had invited ten people several days ahead and then completely forgot they were coming. That morning they called to ask what time to come. I sprang into action, first setting the dining-room table with champagne grapes, Royal Ann cherries, which were then in season, and some pretty peaches in Steuben bowls.

Rumanian antipasto (see Chapter Nine) was the appetizer. For a first course I made vichyssoise and saved the hollowed-out potato skins in the freezer to serve it in. The second course was a ham, cheese and jalapeño pepper tamale pie cut in squares. The vegetables were french-cut green beans laced through lime rings, and semolina with mushrooms and onions. The salad was Belgian endive and pecans.

The main course was Bagueta bass, from Mexican waters around Mazatlán, in zucchini sauce. It's a moist fish that you can't get all the time, but I have made the same dish using ling cod, which is the closest thing to Bagueta bass. It's very pretty to look at and works equally well as a first course, using smaller pieces of fish.

## BAGUETA BASS IN ZUCCHINI SAUCE

8 serving-size pieces Bagueta bass or ling cod
White cornmeal
Salt, pepper, paprika to taste
¼ cup (½ stick) butter
¼ cup olive oil
1 large onion, chopped
¼ bell pepper, diced fine
Fresh garlic, pressed (optional)
8 small tomatoes, skins on, chopped
2 stems fresh basil, chopped
3 tiny zucchini, sliced *very* thin

Dredge fish in cornmeal and season with salt, pepper and paprika. Set aside. Melt butter in skillet; add olive oil; sauté onion and pepper, with garlic if desired. Add tomatoes and simmer for 10 minutes. Add chopped basil. Put the zucchini slices in at the last minute and leave only long enough for them to be heated through (they should still be crunchy).

In a skillet brown fish 1½ minutes on each side. Put pieces in baking pan, cover with sauce and heat through in a preheated 375° F. oven.

Put a sprig of fresh basil on top of each piece and serve with a half lemon wrapped in cheesecloth. Serves 8.

For dessert I had frozen chocolate crêpes with hot Kahlua sauce poured over the top, and fresh raspberries with sugared walnuts.

After it was all over, I told my friends I had forgotten they were coming.

Here are four disasters you might anticipate and be able to do something about:

1. *Complaining neighbors.* As I mentioned earlier, invite those neighbors with whom you're friendly, but inform all near neighbors in advance that you are having a party and you hope the noise will not disturb them. Always be a good neighbor and try to keep your noise level down, so as not to bother anyone's sleep. And when *they* have parties, be just as tolerant of their noise as you expect them to be of yours.

2. One source of loud noise, of course, is *drunken guests.* If the offender is your husband's boss or the guest of honor, you almost always have to live with it, unless you know him or her very well. If guests get very drunk during the cocktail hour tell them they can't sit at the table. Try to deal with drunks in private, and do everything you can to get them to lie down, drink coffee or go home. If somebody

comes into your house already drunk, summon up the strength to tell him to leave.

3. *No shows.* If you are expecting guests who haven't called to say they'll be late, and you ready to eat, take the place settings off the table. It's unpleasant to have empty places at the table.

4. If they do arrive, as *latecomers,* put their places back on the table—you do always have enough food. If they never show at all and if you still feel friendly, call the next day and say, "It was a really special dinner; I saved you a plate. Come over and get it."

14

PRECEDING PAGES: *A close look at a lovely place setting—and one idea for how to serve caviar.*

# HINTS, SHORT CUTS AND CROWD PLEASERS

Catering by Milton," which is still the formal name of my business, is apparently somewhat different from catering by anybody else. I have my own idiosyncrasies and trademarks (like my Peanut Butter sauce —but don't look for the recipe here because we plan to market it soon). So my hints for entertaining, like my philosophy of party giving, are individual. Some are serious work savers, though they won't all save money (i.e., three dramatic ways to serve caviar on page 199).

## Hints

1. I'm not a great believer in sauces, except, of course, on desserts. If you buy good cuts of meat you don't need sauces. Make sure your meat is choice or even prime. For special cuts, such as a butterflied

fillet of lamb, don't be timid about giving instructions to the butcher. And don't hesitate to ask him to weigh the meat, charge you the price, and then trim the fat off. It saves you trouble later.

2. Roast beef has to sit at least 5 minutes before you slice it. If you slice the beef while it's too hot it will oxidize, and although it is rare it will look well done. If you have to slice the meat in the kitchen, undercook it very slightly so it will look rare on the platter. If you are slicing it at the table the guests will see that it is rare before it hits their plates.

3. Fish doesn't take very long to cook, and the most likely problem is overcooking, so watch it very carefully. A sure test for the doneness of fish is to take a fork and lift up the middle of the fish's belly. Pull away, and if a little piece comes out easily, the fish is done.

I'm not a fish lover, though I love the *idea* of fish and the possibilities for the presentation of it. I've only cooked fish with the bone out, but I do have a recipe for a whole baked salmon that can feed up to 18 people.

## FRESH BAKED SALMON

> 10-pound fresh Chinook salmon, deboned and butterflied, with the head off
>    but the tail still on
> 1 cup (2 sticks) butter, melted
> 4 tablespoons dried celery
> 4 tablespoons dried onion
> 1 tablespoon dill weed
> Paprika, pepper, seasoned salt to taste
> 1 pint sauterne

Open the salmon and stuff the fish's belly with half the butter, the celery and onion and spices to taste. Sprinkle a bit of the sauterne inside the fish before closing it. On top of the closed fish put more seasoned salt, pepper and paprika, the remaining butter, and brush with more wine. Wrap the fish loosely in aluminum foil in which sits the balance of the wine for steaming. Put into a preheated 400° F. oven for 30 minutes, checking once during cooking (but not turning).

4. Some people, particularly Americans, like their coffee right away although it's bad manners for a guest to ask for it. While they're waiting for dessert it *is* perfectly okay to give your guests a cup of coffee. It also gives you more preparation time for dessert. Things like this are getting a little more relaxed. Maybe at a state dinner they shouldn't serve coffee before dessert, but just about everywhere else it's fine. A party is to enjoy. If you or someone else is dying for coffee, why not have it?

5. Entertaining books always said that you had to wait until everybody was served before eating. Bull. Why should you let the food get cold? Often today the hostess won't even be the first one served, so you can't wait for her to begin. As soon as you get the food, start eating it. America is the only country that waits for the food to get cold till all are served, and you can see the fallacy in it. It's ridiculous. It's a changing world in that respect, and if people are in doubt about beginning to eat, the hostess should insist on it.

6. By the same token, the hostess doesn't necessarily sit at the head of the table if I can help it. Put the guest of honor at the head and you as host or hostess sit on the side. That is far more cordial.

7. If the cocktail hour—*one* hour—has gone by and your food is ready, serve dinner even if latecomers have yet to arrive. When they do they'll come to the table a little bit embarrassed and next time maybe they will get there on time. Don't ruin your meal because of impolite guests. Sit down and eat.

Sometimes accidents do happen and if they've called to say that they are running late and you can hold dinner up for a little while, do. But if you can't hold it up, they'll understand. You can heat it up for them whenever they do arrive. But lateness of any kind can ruin your seating for conversation and you may have to hastily rearrange your table.

8. Soufflés don't wait for late guests, but I have one that can wait a little bit: it can be held up by turning the oven down. This works for many types of soufflés. This a technique to be used with your favorite starch souffle (not dessert soufflé). I put more eggs into it and I put more filling into it. My soufflés are not so wet, but they stand up and cut out like angel food cake. It's because I use sour cream instead of cream sauce. Sour cream is already thick, so you don't have to worry about thickening it. I just take butter, eggs, sour cream and cream cheese and beat the hell out of it before folding the cooked filling into it. Then fold egg whites into it. Butter the soufflé dish, pour the mixture in and bake it. That girl will stand up. The cream cheese and sour cream together seem to act as a stabilizer. This works for cheese, noodle, spinach, rice, egg barley, semolina, broccoli and some dessert soufflés. It works very well with chocolate, but not with strawberries. I developed the soufflé just by playing with it; if it had been difficult I never would have made it. Using this recipe, we've been able to serve soufflés to 200 or 300 people.

9. When you find a supplier you like, whether it's the local ice cream parlor, a restaurant, an Italian corner grocery, stick with it. You'll always know that you're getting the best, even if it costs a little more. A delicatessen in East Orange, New Jersey, flies in their smoked salmon to me once a week. Of all the smoked salmon I've ever had, theirs is the best. They preslice it and put it into a cryovac container, and it's delivered right to my door. I use my weekly order of smoked salmon for various parties. The deli in East Orange also makes marvelous little stuffed cabbage leaves, potato knishes, and kosher salamis. Whenever I find something really special like that I try to establish a rapport so they'll send it to me in large enough quantities to make it worth their while.

# Short Cuts

10. An easy orange-cranberry glaze for duck or chicken is made from one 8-ounce jar of currant jelly, one 2½-ounce can of frozen orange juice and one 1-pound can of whole cranberry sauce. Grate some orange rind and a green apple into it. Brown your chicken or duck and put this melted glaze over it. Pour on a little wine and then put the bird back in the oven. Cover it.

11. To cook chicken ahead when you're going to get home just before your guests arrive, half cook it the day before. First, sprinkle the chicken with salt, pepper and paprika. Then brown it lightly in a little olive oil. Pour off the grease. In the browning pan put some onion, a little brown sugar, lemon juice and a little wine and throw that over the chicken or duck. Then cook rice, but again not all the way through. Make a bed of rice, put the duck or chicken on top of it. Put peaches, pineapple, or apricots on top of that, depending on your taste, and put it in the refrigerator until you're ready to reheat. It maintains its freshness and won't get dried out. It takes 10 minutes the day before to brown the meat and undercook the rice, and about 30 minutes the night of the dinner to reheat.

12. Strawberries must be soaked to get the sand out of them, but if you soak them even a day ahead they will fizzle out in the refrigerator. However, if you soak them and put them on a paper towel to drain, then place them in a jar with a tight lid, they will keep up to *five* days in the refrigerator.

13. Similarly, shrimp that has already been cooked and cleaned will dissolve even twenty-four hours ahead of serving if left as is in the refrigerator. But if you marinate it first (pick your marinade according to how you plan to serve the shrimp later, but I would use a garlic, oil, vinegar, salt and pepper marinade) it will keep up to sixty-two hours ahead of your party—in the refrigerator, of course.

14. An easy way to serve oysters, rather than on the half shell, is to buy fresh oysters in a pint or quart jar, and put them in small sake cups that you can buy cheaply at an import house. Serve them with a demitasse spoon and your favorite dressing, horseradish or whatever.

# Crowd Pleasers

15. Buy nuts and bolts from the hardware store, one pair for each couple coming to your dinner. Give the nuts to the women, the bolts to the men, and ask them to find the proper fit. When they have they have also found their dinner partners. It's a little bit naughty, but nice.

16. For a party I had at my house I bought green plants for a dollar apiece at the dime store and replanted them in large wineglasses. I bought beautiful little orchids in tubes for fifty cents a bloom and wired them to the plants so they looked like orchid plants. It cost next to nothing because I used my own wineglasses. I took the orchids out at the end of the evening and gave them to the ladies to take home. For a buck or two there are lots of things like that you can do; a pretty look for a table can come from just last-minute stopping off at the nursery on the way home from the grocery store.

17. When the famous French chef Paul Bocuse came to Los Angeles, several local chefs were asked to contribute a specialty to a party in his honor. Since I'm not a gourmet cook I thought long and hard about it. It was before Thanksgiving, and at that time of year there is naturally an abundance of turkey testicles. Tom turkeys are castrated and the testicles are usually thrown away—as a consumer of turkeys buying one in a grocery store, you never see this part of the bird. Since I am a believer in ecology and the motto "Waste not, want not," I decided to make use of these items for the Bocuse party. After all, pigs' testicles are served as "mountain oysters."

I batter-fried them in a mixture of egg, flour, baking powder, seasoned salt, paprika and milk, and served them on toothpicks with a mustard and catsup sauce on the side. Some people thought they were shrimp, but they became a very popular item and I often do them around the holidays.

18. Caviar is served for birthdays and anniversaries, some weddings and very elegant sit-down dinners. The American domestic caviar costs something like one fourth the price of the Russian or Iranian caviar and is really quite good. One way to serve it is to bake a potato for each person, scoop them out, then whip the potatoes in sweet butter and a little onion. Put the potato mixture back in the shells, then load them with caviar and serve with a knife and fork. Pass sour cream around the table. It's a delicious first course.

Another way to serve caviar makes use of covered soup bowls, which people don't often use even when they have them. I use soup bowls for many things; if you've got them use them. Create something for them. Set your table with all your pretty things and then create something that uses each dish and glass. You can use soup bowls as salad bowls, or as finger bowls with a slice of lemon in them. Use soup bowls for seafood cocktails in ice, with a shot glass in the center to hold the sauce.

For the soup bowls I got individual tins of caviar, an ounce and a half each. I filled the bowls with crushed ice, put the tin on top of the ice with lemon and parsley on the side, then put the cover on the bowl. We passed sour cream seasoned with onion and hot, thick French toast, made of egg bread and fried in sweet butter. So each person had his or her own little tin of caviar, which was extremely chichi. You hear all kinds of "oooohs" and "aaaahs" when your guests open those bowls to find the caviar. With the price of even domestic caviar, you would obviously reserve this for a fairly small special group.

A third way to use caviar is on blinis, Russian style. We cook the blinis individually the size of a quarter, on the spot. I put one teaspoon of caviar on a blini, then put another blini on top of that, then sour cream, grated onion and chopped egg. So it's like a little sandwich. We put just two of those on a small plate with a little cocktail fork and a linen napkin. It's very elegant and some people naturally ask for more. Put them off by saying, "I don't want to ruin your dinner."

15

# FINISHING TOUCHES

**W**hether you are a professional party giver or a novice you can forget some detail or other. No matter how carefully I plan a party, or how carefully you read this book and map out your party, there will always be something that needs to be dealt with at the last minute. When I arrive a couple of hours before the start of one of my parties I take a broad view right away. The eye just picks up something that is not quite right. It's like a sixth sense with me, and you should try to develop it. I will see mismatched silver or a buffet table—even before the food is put on it—that just isn't going to work. I don't care how diligent someone is about writing everything down, invariably something turns out slightly wrong.

Last-Minute Check List for Entire Evening

1. Count your place settings to make sure that you have the right number.

2. The last minute before the guests arrive a host or hostess should especially check for all the implements that will be needed to serve and eat. Check the menu again to see what silverware should be on the table and how it should be lined up.

Don't trust your mind to remember those little details. You've got too much to think about with the food. Make a list:

3. Does anything need to be added to the table, (which was set the day or week before)? Are the flowers on the table? Salt, pepper, butter?

4. Is the atmosphere arranged? Are there sufficient ashtrays in place around the room? Candles, flowers, candy, nuts? Is the music ready to begin?

5. Drinks—what are you serving and where in the house? Do you have enough ice? Enough glasses? Are the mixes, lemons and limes, cocktail onions out on the bar or serving area?

6. Are *you* and your bathroom ready for your guests? Are you bathed, dressed, in full make-up? More important, are you confident about your party?

7. Is the food preparation on schedule? Are there any last-minute instructions for your help/caterer?

No matter how modest your table, it makes a statement, and people will remember that statement. If there is just a little something extra from *you,* people pick it up immediately. Start with the entertaining ideas in this book, but then use your own initiative. Find a little figurine and work it into your table décor. Scatter some fall leaves, if in season, down the table, if that seems appropriate. When you're shopping for the food, maybe you'll find a little Seckel pear and make an insertion in it to hold a little place card. Or take one rose and tie it to a name card.

If you're having a "Sweet Sixteen" party, make use of sugar cubes. Put loose sugar on your tablecloth like sand, and make little garden walls of sugar cubes. Add little bonsai trees, little paper oriental parasols, flower petals and a Japanese figurine. That's a simple Sweet Sixteen centerpiece. Everybody's got sugar in the cabinet.

You have got to get away from store-bought table decorations. The markets and stationery stores are full of things for people who can't—or won't—use their imaginations. The nice thing to do is to use what you've got and do it yourself.

There are at least thirty-two different ways to fold napkins (see a few of them in the color section), and how we fold them and where we put them depends on the look we want for the table. Sometimes arrange them in the wineglasses, sometimes fold them simply at the left side of the plate, sometimes use a napkin ring. Napkin rings can be used for as many as two hundred people, to carry out a motif. I've used mirrored napkin rings, and others that were flutes for the guests to take home. For showers I've used napkin rings of grosgrain ribbon.

I have used double napkins to enhance the table: one is for dinner, the other is for dessert. One is in lace, the other is a solid color, so that when they are folded together you know you've got two.

Although I usually prefer to stay in the kitchen, or at least on the periphery of each of the parties that I cater, sometimes I go out on the floor and pass hors d'oeuvres myself just to see what's going on. You as host or hostess, of course, are always right in the thick of things, but throughout the evening you will need to consciously check up on not only your paid helpers but also your guests. You will want to be sure that they are getting everything they need but still behaving themselves. What people represent, or how much money they have, doesn't necessarily mean they have good manners. That's something that every guest has to work on himself. But a good host or hostess can lead a lot of people in the right direction.

One truly unforgettable finishing touch for any party is the presentation of a dish that is universally regarded as difficult to produce. Such a dish is the perfect pork roast. Here is one that will help make your dinner party the party of the year.

# PERFECT PORK ROAST

**Whole loin of pork, about 8–10 pounds**
**Garlic salt, seasoned salt, pepper, paprika, dry mustard, olive oil**

Rub oil and seasonings all over pork loin and roast in a preheated 400° F. oven for 45 minutes; then turn oven down to 350° F. and cook for another hour. Cover with pork glaze and serve with cabbage slaw in orange shells. Serves 16 to 20.

### PORK GLAZE

**Three green onions (scallions), green part only**
**Grated rind of 1 lemon**
**Grated rind of 1 orange**
**2 (25-ounce) jars prunes**
**1 (16-ounce) can pineapple chunks, chopped up**
**½ pound (2 sticks) butter**
**½ pound brown sugar**
**4 tablespoons Worcestershire sauce**
**4 tablespoons A-1 sauce**
**4 tablespoons teriyaki sauce**
**½ cup red wine**
**1 egg**
**Salt and pepper**

Combine all ingredients in a large saucepan and cook on top of the stove, over medium heat, until the sauce cooks down (about 45 minutes).

## CABBAGE SLAW IN ORANGE SHELLS

2 heads cabbage

3 cups sugar

2 pints sour cream

1 teaspoon seasoned salt

3 tablespoons celery seed

¼ teaspoon white pepper

Core and shred cabbage, sprinkle with sugar and put on a large plate. Put another plate on top and leave overnight. Squeeze juice out of cabbage and mix sour cream and spices into it (don't be afraid to mix thoroughly). Serve in half orange shells.

By now you are probably ready to tackle a major party but are still concerned—and rightly so—about your budget. Here are two parties that anyone can do within the budgets outlined.

# $1,000 Garden Party for 100

One 20-foot buffet table with French blue linens; white wicker baskets filled with spikes of blue delphiniums, pink rubrum lilies, pink roses and white larkspur.

One 20-foot white canopy over the table; the poles are wrapped in white and garlanded with smilax.

One 10-foot buffet table and ten-foot canopy decorated the same way, for sweets and coffee.

White umbrella tables for guests to sit at, with blue cloths, poles wrapped in white and garlanded with smilax. Centerpieces around poles are made up of pink tea roses, bouvardia and maidenhair fern. Pink napkins are folded into wineglasses.

## Menu

*Boned apricot chicken*
*Noodles with poppy seeds and almonds*
*Cold poached salmon and dill sauce*
*Sweet and sour cucumbers*
*Cold asparagus vinaigrette*
*Green bean, walnut and water chestnut salad*
*White fruit salad*
*Assorted cheeses and crackers*
*Grissini*
*Rolls and butter*

## Sweet Table

*Chilled melon balls with mint*
*Wet chocolate cake*
*Lemon schaum torte with hot lemon sauce*
*Fresh raspberries*
*Crème brûlée*
*Chocolate parisian cream torte*
*Assorted cookies*
*Coffee*

# $5,000 Christmas Party for 50

Five 60-inch round tables
Five red cloths, 120-inch round, to the floor
Gold bentwood chairs with red velvet seats
Five round centerpieces of holly, red carnations, popcorn balls and candy canes. Put five 24-inch red tapers in each.
50 red napkins
Buffet table with centerpiece of roast geese in a Della Robbia wreath of holly, lady apples, Seckel pears, chestnuts and tangerines. Decorate the rest of the table with pine boughs and cones, a red cloth, tall red tapers with garlands of holly and red carnations.

## *Menu*

*Rack of lamb*
*Baked whitefish stuffed with zucchini and corn*
*Mint-glazed poached pears*
*Barley soufflé*
*Sliced beefsteak tomatoes with artichoke bottoms stuffed with cucumber relish*
*Marinated mushrooms*
*Brie cheese and crackers*
*Croissants and butter*
*Desserts are on a sideboard:*
*hot persimmon pudding with custard sauce,*
*double-crust walnut pie, stem strawberries and chocolate fondue,*
*Christmas cookies, gingerbread house, coconut cake shaped like a Santa,*
*chocolate yule log with mocha cream, chestnut mousse with toasted hazel nuts,*
*croquem bouche*
*Put coffee and liqueurs on the same sideboard*

# $165,000 Fantasy Ball for 165

This party was given by Mr. William Weinberg, owner of the Kahala Hilton Hotel in Honolulu, in honor of his wife Hermine's fortieth birthday, on April 12, 1980.

The invitations were in silver boxes, wrapped in white chantilly lace, ribbon and artificial emeralds and amethysts. They announced a Jewel Ball, in black tie and gowns (no evening pajamas), were hand-delivered, and had a return card inside.

When the guests arrived the parking boys were in white tie and tails and tall silk hats. At the door there was a long table with sixteen silver vases filled with ten or eleven flowers each. Each vase had a different variety and color of flower. To each flower was attached a card with a name written in the color of a gemstone. That told the guests which table was theirs.

Cocktails and buffet hors d'oeuvres were served in the Weinberg house itself. Hors d'oeuvres included: pâté; crab claws; Alaskan crab legs; shrimp; Scotch salmon with cream cheese, onion and capers; tiny potato pancakes with fresh caviar and sour cream; baby lamb chops; tiny truffle pâté with toast; spinach pies with Swiss cheese and phyllo dough; melon and prosciutto.

The hors d'oeuvre table was covered in a lavender and lace cloth and had a huge centerpiece of white phalaenopsis orchids and sterling silver roses. Lavender tulips were sprinkled down the table, along with crystal amethyst art objects, and Hermine's antique amethyst perfume bottles.

All drinks were served by waiters—literally anything the guests wanted. The soft background music came from a Steinway grand and a string quartet. That was in addition to the violins on either side of the doorway that ushered the guests in.

Dinner was under a tent that covered the entire back yard. The tent poles were wrapped in white satin and the whole top of the tent was done in fresh peppers sprayed white. At the very top was a wheel of soft lights, alternating red, green, lavender, blue and white. A snow-white carpet covered the lawn. At the base of the garden were tulips, blue and pink hydrangeas, exotic greenery and stuffed peacocks.

There was a lighted dance floor and a full dance orchestra on a stage above it. The guests sat in all-white spindle-back chairs, with silver lamé seats. The tables were keyed to various jewels: an emerald-green cloth and napkins, green orchids, bells of Ireland, green cymbidiums; ruby-red table linen and red roses and tulips; diamond-white cloth and napkins, white roses, phalaenopsis and lilies of the valley; sapphire-blue, with iris, cornflowers, delphinium and blue violets, etc. There were so many clumps of different varieties of white orchids it looked like wisteria.

A waiter was assigned to each table to ask what each guest wanted. The menu was a choice of charcoal-broiled chateaubriand, crisp orange duck or baked Puget Sound salmon, with asparagus in lemon butter; barley, mushrooms and onions. The waiters brought cheese and fruit and frozen lemon ice in a real lemon skin. This was followed by frozen chocolate truffles. Then the guests, led by the host and hostess, walked to the garden, where a five-tiered birthday cake topped by a crown of jewels was served with fresh raspberries. There was also an entire show which included members from a local ballet company and a professional blues singer.

The favors for this fabulous evening were sterling silver boxes lined with red velvet and filled with silver almonds. Each box was engraved with a guest's name.

(There was no first course, because of all the hors d'oeuvres— certain principles of entertaining apply to any party.) The wines were Château Lafite Rothschild 1966, Puligny-Montrachet 1971 and Louis Roederer Cristal champagne with dessert.

As you can see from the photographs, this is the kind of party I waited twenty-eight years to do, and I enjoyed it almost more than any other I've done. But my basic belief, expressed throughout this book, remains the same: no matter how many or few the guests, how plain or elegant the food, entertaining, once you put your mind to it, is simple.

My final thought is that I am a very religious man; the Bible says "For where two or three are gathered in my name, there am I in the midst of them." Well, you and this book make two . . .

# INDEX

kosher, 162–63
salt-free meals, 161–62
vegetarianism (*see also*
Vegetarian meals), 163–64
disasters, coping with, 181–84
equipment and supplies needed (*see
also* Kitchen), 12–13, 46–54
ethnic cuisine (*see also* names of
specific ethnic groups), 137–51
quantities to buy and prepare, 7,
54–55, 56
catered party, 85
second servings
keeping warm, 21
planning for, 54
short cuts, 197–98
soufflés, 196
suppliers, keeping in with, 196
wine cookery, 69–70, 72
Costs
catered parties, 84–88
charity parties, cutting costs for, 88
entertaining at home vs. going to a
restaurant, 7
help, hired, 80, 81
Costume parties, 124–25
*Around the World in Eighty Days,*
125
Country fair, 125
Crab, curried, and served in a papaya,
111
Crème brûlée, improvised variation
of, 182
Crème fraîche, 171

Date
changing, 41
choosing the, 15
and sending out of invitations,
39–40, 41
Debutante parties, 126
Decorations
American Indian party, 149
autumn, 30
debutante party, 126
candles, 5–6, 57
Christmas table, 105
fantasy ball for 165, $165,000,
210–11
floral, 5, 30, 57, 198
outdoors, 87–88
fruit and vegetables, 5, 13, 14, 30,

51
garden party, 127, 207–8
Greek dinner, 27
imaginative and appropriate, 204–5
plants, 5, 13–14, 57, 198
for salad bar, 156
Scottish party, 150
Southern American theme, 150
"Sweet Sixteen" party, 205
table, 5–6, 13–14, 30, 59, 198
using what you have, 12
Dessert parties, 126
Desserts, 169
apple charlotte, 171
blueberry pie or tarts
crust and lining basic, 171–72
filling, 172
brownie pudding, baked in
flowerpot, 122
brunch, 122
celestial fruit, 174
cheesecake
pashka recipe variation, 173
pumpkin, 110–11
Chinese menu, 151
chocolate mousse, frozen, 174–76
and coffee, serving, 195
crème brûlée, improvised variation
of, 182
disasters, coping with, 182–84
doughnuts, heart-shaped, for
Valentine's Day, 111
figs and crème fraîche, 170–71
Fondue Au Chocolate, 174–75
fudge cake served in flowerpot,
122
ice cream, 170
sundaes, cart with toppings for,
172–73
torte, 170
quantities to prepare
sunshine cake, 173
table settings for, 52
wines to serve with
champagne, 72
sherry, 72
sweet white, 72
wines used in preparation of, 70
Dietary restrictions, 161
dieters, 164–65
filet of sole, 250-calorie, 165
kosher, 162–63

216

INDEX

number of drinks and size of bottle, 56

plastic glasses for, 30

quantities to provide, 56

serving equipment renting or borrowing, 53, 54

wines (see also Wines)
  cocktail, 22, 67
  dinner, 21, 62–72

Luncheon party, games for a, 32

Maids, hired
  duties, 79, 80–81
  firing, 81
  sources
    employment agencies, 79, 81
    restaurants or diners, local, 81
  uniforms
    own, 79, 80
    special, 81–82

Mancini, Henry, moving party, 130

Manners
  eating when served, 195
  good guest, 82–83
  seating the guest of honor, 195

Margot Factor's fried sauerkraut, 143

McCartney (Paul)/Wings party, 56–57, 85–86

Meats (see also specific meats)
  buying, 193–94
  kosher, 162
  for salad bar, 157
  sauces not needed for, 193

Menus (see also Cooking for parties; recipes)
  American Indian, 149
  appetizers, 29, 30
  brunch, 121–22
    Italian, 140
  children's parties, 123
    hero sandwich, 101
  Chinese, 151
  Christmas party
    for 50, $5,000, 209
    old-fashioned, 105
  corned beef from delicatessen, 28–29
  Easter party, Russian, 106, 107
  ethnic cuisine (see also specific ethnic groups)
    economical, 137–51
    wines to go with, 68–69

fantasy ball for 165, $165,000, 210–11

fettuccine party, 4–5

first party, 8–13

garden party, 127
  $1,000 for 100, 207–8

Greek, 147–48
  buffet dinner, 25–26
  wines to serve with, 68

gumbo party, 10–12

Halloween, 108

high tea, 128–29

hors d'oeuvres, 22, 29–30, 54–55

Hungarian, 143–44

$100 dinner for ten, 23–25
  dinner, easy, 8–10
  wines to serve with, 68

Italian, 137–42

kosher, 162–63

Mexican, 145–47
  Sangría to serve with, 68–69

midnight breakfast, 126

one-dish, 4–5, 21, 27–28

Rumanian, 143–44

Scottish, 150

Southern American, 150–51

Spanish, 145–47
  Sangría to serve with, 68–69

sparkling Burgundy, 66

supper, 21–29

Thanksgiving, 109–11

Valentine's Day party, 111

wines to go with (see also Wines), 66–69

Yom Kippur, 115

Mexican
  cuisine, 145–47
    arroz con pollo (with shrimp), 145–46
    empanadas, 146
    party theme, uniforms and, 81
    potato tortillas, 146–47
    salad to go with, 156
    Sangría to serve with, 68–69

Milton Williams' gumbo, 11

Milton's basic spaghetti sauce with clams, 138–39
  variations, 139

Mixed drinks, see Cocktails; Liquor

Moussaka, 26

Moving parties, 130

Music